THE VICTORIAN
MASTER CRIMINAL

THE
VICTORIAN
MASTER CRIMINAL

DAVID C. HANRAHAN

To Margaret, Aisling and Michael
for everything

First published 2016

The History Press
The Mill, Brimscombe Port
Stroud, Gloucestershire, GL5 2QG
www.thehistorypress.co.uk

© David C. Hanrahan, 2016

The right of David C. Hanrahan to be identified as the Author
of this work has been asserted in accordance with the
Copyright, Designs and Patents Act 1988.

British Library Cataloguing in Publication Data.
A catalogue record for this book is available from the British Library.

ISBN 978 0 7509 6297 1

Typesetting and origination by The History Press
Printed in Great Britain

Contents

Part 3

Part 4

Part 1

The Murder of Constable Cock

In the general area of Whalley Range, Manchester, just after midnight in the early minutes of 2 August 1876, police constables Nicholas Cock and James Beanland were doing their normal nightly rounds. The area that they were patrolling was regarded as one of their more 'respectable' suburbs, with its array of impressive houses and gardens. The two constables had split up for a little while and Constable Cock was walking with his friend, a law student named John Massey Simpson.

Constable Cock and John Massey Simpson met Constable Beanland beside a local landmark known as the 'jutting-stone at West Point', where the three men stood in conversation for some five minutes. As they chatted, they saw a man walking from Upper Chorlton Road. 'Who is that man?' Constable Beanland asked, peering into the darkness. His companions looked, but not being able to see much did not answer. The man in question seemed slightly unsettled by the sight of the two constables and after a short hesitation turned up Seymour Grove. At one point he had been only 10–12 yards away from them, but in the darkness of the night neither the constables nor John Massey Simpson could make out more than the barest outline of the man's figure, the brown overcoat that he had on, the 'pot hat' on his head and the slight stoop in the way that he walked.[1]

Something about the manner in which he had glanced at the constables, just briefly, before walking off 'at a quick pace', attracted their attention sufficiently for them to follow him.[2] As the constables moved to investigate the matter further, Mr Massey Simpson parted company with them and proceeded home along Upper Chorlton Road.

As the policemen walked up Seymour Grove, the mysterious man was nowhere to be seen. On reaching the property of Mr Gratrix, however, they noticed that the garden gate was not closed correctly. Constable Beanland entered the garden and went up to the house to investigate; Constable Cock waited on the road. Beanland checked the rear door to the house and found that it was locked securely. There was nothing suspicious. He had a quick look through the windows and everything inside seemed fine too.

At the same time two working men, Abraham Ellison and William Morrell, were passing by on horse-drawn carts. Both men, who were travelling together, noticed the small, familiar figure of Constable Cock or the 'Little Bobby' as he was known locally, being only 5ft 8in tall.[3] They saw Cock standing looking up Seymour Grove. The men had gone no more than 10 or 12 yards further when their horses were startled by the sound of two loud bangs. They recognised these as the sounds of gunshots.

John Massey Simpson heard them too. Realising what they were and concerned for the well-being of his two constable friends, he ran back towards them. As he did so, he saw Ellison and Morrell struggling to get their spooked horses under control. The men had just managed to calm the horses when they saw Constable Cock stagger from Seymour Grove and fall to the ground.

Constable Beanland, still inside the garden, had turned back towards Mr Gratrix's gate when he heard the shots coming from the other side of the garden wall. He saw two accompanying flashes of bright light. To his horror, he heard his colleague call out in distress, 'Murder, murder, I'm shot, I'm shot'.[4] Beanland ran to the road and was the first to reach the Little Bobby. He found Cock lying on the ground, his head leaning against a wall. He could see fresh bruising emerging on his colleague's forehead and right cheek. He raised Cock into a sitting position against the wall and said to him, 'Oh, Cock, whatever is the matter?'[5] Constable Beanland began to whistle furiously for assistance.

Ellison, Morrell and John Massey Simpson came running. Another constable, William Ewen, who had been on duty nearby, arrived in response to the sound of the shots and the frenzied whistling of his colleague. Realising that the bleeding constable's condition was very serious, the men loaded him up onto one of the horse carts. 'Do you know who shot you?' Constable Ewen asked the injured Cock as they did so.

'No,' the Little Bobby replied, adding simply, 'They have done for me this time.'[6]

The men rushed the injured constable to the house of Dr John Dill. By now the concerned group had been joined by Police Sergeant Moses Thompson. Thompson also inquired of Constable Cock, a number of times, whether he knew who his assailant was but by now the wounded man was unable to give any cogent reply. Dr Dill examined the patient and noted that he had a wound under his right nipple that was bleeding profusely. The doctor probed the wound. As the doctor conducted this painful investigation, Cock spoke only once more, saying, 'Leave me a be. Oh, Frank, you are killing me.'[7] There was no one in the room called Frank.

The doctor knew as soon as he had examined Constable Cock's wound that there was little chance of him surviving the night. He was barely alive by the time Police Superintendent James Bent arrived on the scene; the superintendent had been awoken from his sleep, such was the gravity of the situation. Constable Cock died about forty minutes after being brought to the doctor's house.[8] He was 26 years of age and had only been a constable for eight months.[9]

Dr Dill carried out a post-mortem examination on his body. 'There were no other injuries but the [gunshot] wound and the bruises on the face. The bullet had passed through the lung and lodged under the fourth rib. A piece of bone had penetrated through the lung.'[10] The doctor removed a conical shaped bullet from the muscles of Constable Cock's spine, where it had become lodged.[11]

As those present struggled to come to terms with what had happened to the young policeman, Superintendent James Bent believed that he already knew who was responsible for this heinous crime and he was determined to make the perpetrators pay.[12]

A Swift Arrest

Police Superintendent James Bent was a respected member of the community; an experienced officer who had shown himself to be both tough and compassionate. Bent had enjoyed a long and distinguished career in law enforcement.

Born in Eccles in 1828, he had become a constable in 1848. Law enforcement was to become his lifelong career. By 1868, through hard work and dedication he had risen to the rank of superintendent of the Manchester Police Division. He was understandably aggrieved, shocked and angered by this callous murder of a young, conscientious constable doing his duty. He was determined to act decisively and promptly in the arrest and punishment of those responsible for the crime.

Bent was not an unduly insensitive man. In fact, according to himself, when he was young he feared that he might be 'too timid' to ever achieve his aim of becoming a constable.[13] However, over the years, as necessitated by the rigours of the job, he managed to develop a tougher side to his personality. He had found himself in many dangerous and violent situations and was nearly killed on more than one occasion. During one particularly bad incident in Miles Platting he received a number of serious blows to the head and his attacker had even tried 'to burn out his tongue with a heated iron'.[14] Bent survived the attack, albeit suffering from adverse health effects afterwards.

Yet, for all his violent encounters with those involved in crime, Superintendent Bent managed to maintain a sympathy for the poor of Manchester. During one particularly severe winter he became concerned about the suffering of the less well-off children in his area, and in order to ease their plight he established a soup kitchen to feed them at Old Trafford Police Station.

He continued the soup kitchen for years afterwards, with the assistance of his wife, and probably saved thousands of children from starvation.[15] The soup kitchen also helped to engender a degree of trust between the police and a group of troubled children who, up to this point, had regarded authority figures with nothing but fear and disdain. The children helped by the soup kitchen even became known locally as 'Bent's Children'.[16]

The fervour and determination that was evident in Bent's investigation of Constable Cock's murder was no doubt driven both by a fierce loyalty to his men and a revulsion towards the act that had been committed against one of them. The superintendent became convinced that he knew who was responsible for the murder. It was common knowledge that Constable Cock was not an altogether popular figure with many of the people living in his area due to his overzealous attitude to enforcing the law.

The police superintendent was aware, in particular, of three brothers in the locality with whom Cock had developed a highly acrimonious relationship of late. Constable Cock had informed Superintendent Bent about a number of violent threats that had been made against him by three Irish brothers called John, William and Frank Habron, or Hebron.[17] The bad feeling between Cock and the Habron brothers had come about as a result of the constable's attempt to prosecute them for drunkenness and disorderly conduct.

The incident in question occurred after a night of drinking engaged in by William and Frank at a local bar called Lloyd's Hotel. They both became inebriated. So much so, in fact, that William decided that he would have to go home to fetch their other brother, John, so he could assist him in getting Frank home. As it happened John was at home that evening because he felt unwell. John went to Lloyd's with William, they collected Frank and walked him home.

Unfortunately, just as they were nearing home, they were approached by three constables, one of whom was Constable Nicholas Cock. Cock grabbed William and Frank by the backs of their collars unceremoniously and said that he was taking them into custody for being drunk and disorderly. This was only avoided by the arrival of the Habrons' boss, Mr Francis Deakin, who persuaded the constables to let his men go to bed instead. Nevertheless, a few days later William and John received legal summonses ordering their appearance in court, instigated by Constable Cock. This infuriated the Habrons, particularly John, who had not drunk any alcohol that day and was being blamed without justification.[18]

William's case was heard before the magistrates on 27 July 1876, only days before Constable Cock's murder and he was fined 5s along with costs. On 1 August, only a few hours before Cock's murder, John's case was dismissed because of the mistaken identity.[19]

According to Superintendent Bent, while all this was going on the Habrons had threatened the life of Constable Cock on a number of occasions. He remembered the words of his now fallen constable. 'They have threatened several times to shoot me within the last few months,' Cock had told him.[20] Superintendent Bent claimed that Cock had even expressed concerns to him on the day of the murder itself. According to the superintendent he had said, 'John Habron has just told me that he will shoot me before twelve o'clock tonight.'[21] Bent had asked Cock if he was afraid, but Cock had told him that he was not. The superintendent, however, thought he was 'a little troubled in his mind' about the threats.[22] To Superintendent Bent it was now clear that the Habrons had followed through on those threats to murder the young constable.

Superintendent James Bent was determined to bring those he believed responsible for Cock's murder to justice. (Trafford Local Studies)

Bent lost no time in acting on his convictions; a few hours after Cock's murder, the superintendent and his men surrounded the property of Mr Deakin where the Habrons lived and worked as nursery farm labourers. John Habron worked as a foreman for Mr Deakin and was highly regarded by his boss.[23]

As he called out for Mr Deakin to answer the door to his house, Bent noticed that a light was lit in the outhouse where the brothers slept. Mr Deakin came to the door and the superintendent, as he claimed later, had a conversation with him during which their employer made a comment that was rather incriminating with regard to at least one of the Habron brothers, 'What is to do, Mr Bent?'

'Cock is shot.'

'Who has done it?'

'Nay, I must ask *you* who has done it.'

'Oh, Dear me. I told them to let it drop, and have no more bother about it. Oh, my God, if it is any of these men it is that young one as he has the most abominable temper of any man I ever knew in my life.'[24]

By 'the young one' Bent took Deakin to mean William Habron. Bent then requested Mr Deakin's assistance with their arrest:

> Will you go quietly to this out building, and let your voice be heard, so that they will know it is you, and then get them to open the door to speak to you, and I will rush into the room. I do not wish you to run any risk, unless your care to do so, but simply to make them believe that it is you at the door and not the police.[25]

At first Deakin was not keen to co-operate in this underhand plot against his employees, but in the face of official pressure he decided to relent.[26] By the time they were ready to approach the outhouse, the light that Bent had noticed earlier had been extinguished. Bent was sure that the light had been on only moments before and, therefore, that the men had not been asleep. The Habrons would always be adamant that there was no light in the outhouse that night. They claimed that as the constables were attempting to surround the building and had approached from different sides, what Bent saw was one of the lanterns held by his own men shining through the windows from the opposite side.[27]

According to Bent, it took three separate knocks and a violent shaking of the door to get the Habrons to open it. Once they did so, the superintendent and his men burst into the single-roomed building where the three brothers had been lying naked in bed.[28] The superintendent's police lantern illuminated the darkness of the primitive outhouse. Bent announced his presence and warned the men against making any resistance. The bed clothes were pulled off and they were ordered to get dressed, one by one, in the same clothes that they had been wearing that evening. As far as the superintendent was concerned 'they did not seem like men that had been asleep'.[29]

Bent told the men to put on their boots; once they had done so, thereby confirming ownership, he took the boots from them for examination.[30] All three pairs of boots were wet, but Bent noticed that William's were especially 'slutchy', or muddy, and had been worn outside in wet ground not long before.[31] They had, of course, been working hard that day out in the muddy ground, just as they did most days. John had been gathering raspberries while his younger brother, William, had been engaged with another labourer called John Cosgrove in the tying of lettuces.[32] Superintendent Bent kept William's boots and gave the others back. The superintendent noticed that William was wearing a pot hat, just like the one that had been worn by the suspicious man who had been observed by his constables near the scene of the murder earlier that night.[33]

John and William admitted that they had been close to the scene of the crime earlier that evening when they had gone for a drink at Lloyd's Hotel and had also frequented another establishment called the Royal Oak. Frank had stayed at home and gone to bed early.

Superintendent Bent had the three men handcuffed and he informed them that they were being arrested for the murder of Constable Cock. As he did so, John Habron said, 'I was in bed at the time'.[34] The superintendent would later make a lot of this off the cuff remark, saying that he had not mentioned the time at which the crime had been committed. The Habrons were all taken to Old Trafford Police Station.

Superintendent Bent personally supervised the examination of the crime scene. It had been guarded until daylight the following morning in a bid to prevent any contamination of the evidence. It did not rain overnight until five o'clock in the morning.[35] Bent became very interested in some footprints that were found on the ground in an area of sand and gravel close to the scene of the murder. There were prints there that had been made by 'two or three pairs of boots', but he became focussed upon one print in particular made by a man walking from the direction of Seymour Grove.[36] He sent to the police station for William Habron's boots and made a print in the ground with William's left boot beside the suspect one. 'I compared William's left boot with that footprint,' he would later say, 'and found it to correspond in every particular.'[37]

Although the Habrons claimed to have been home in bed by 9.30 p.m. on the evening of the murder, the police investigation suggested that they had not actually left the place at which they were drinking until around 10.30 p.m. or even 11.00 p.m. Bent and his men did their utmost to find the one object that, more than anything else, would have ensured a conviction. According to Bent himself, all potential hiding places were painstakingly searched for the weapon that had killed Constable Cock, '… every available means were adopted to recover it. Pits were emptied, drains and ditches were searched …'[38]

Not only did they drain every pool of water on the nursery farm and sift through the mud and the sludge that was left behind, they also 'dug over the wheat field'.[39] The murder weapon was not found. The police conducted another search of Deakin's outhouse, where the Habrons slept, on 3 August. On that occasion they found a cartridge for a gun on the mantelpiece and, inside the pocket of a waistcoat, some percussion caps that could be used to fire a pistol.[40]

During the course of their inquiries the police made contact with a man named Donald McClelland who was a shop assistant at an ironmongers situated across from All Saint's Church on Oxford Road in Manchester. He told them that a customer with an Irish accent had come in asking about ammunition and revolvers on either Monday, 31 July or Tuesday, 1 August. He remembered their conversation well.

'Can I see some cartridges?' the young man had asked him.

'What kind?' replied McClelland.

'Can you show me some?'

'What kind. We keep both pin-fire and central-fire.'

'Show me some out of the window.'

'We have both kinds in the window.'

'I'll go outside and point to the box I want to see.'

The young man pointed out the box that he wanted to see and McClelland brought the box to the counter. 'These are Eley's patent central-fire cartridges, No. 450, for revolvers. Have you got the revolver in your pocket?'

McClelland noticed that the man hesitated before replying, 'No, but I think these are the size. How much are they?'

'Either 3s 3d or 3s 6d the box.'

'Can I have less than a box?'

'No. We cannot break into a box.'

'I can't take a box. I'll have to talk to someone else about it.'

McClelland then showed him a revolver designed to take the cartridges in question. In order to demonstrate this, he placed a cartridge inside the chamber. 'I think that is the size,' the customer said. 'How much is the revolver?'

'35s or 40s. But we have some cheaper, from 10s.'[41]

In the end the man left without buying anything. McClelland told the police, however, that later he thought three cartridges were missing from the box that he had shown the man. Superintendent Bent called on McClelland at the ironmongers and asked him to come down to the station to have a look at a suspect for him. He did so and identified William Habron as his Irish customer.

Notwithstanding such damning evidence and the threats that the Habrons had allegedly made against Constable Cock, local knowledge of the brothers did not seem to back up Superintendent Bent's murderous impression of them. A number of people who knew them well said that they did not regard the brothers as dangerous or violent in any way. In spite of Cock's accusations regarding their disorderly and threatening behaviour, those who worked with them said they were not argumentative men. In fact one co-worker said that on the day of the murder they were particularly 'jovial and glad' since Constable Cock's case against John had just been thrown out of court. One letter-writer to *The Times* described them as 'steady, hardworking fellows' and contrary to the superintendent's opinion of them, 'not "given to drink"'.[42] Other descriptions of them included the words 'decent' and 'quiet' and a local physician said that, in his experience, they were 'peaceable' and 'well-conducted'.

John Habron had been employed by Mr Deakin at his nursery garden for nine years and the other two, William and Frank, had followed him over from Ireland and had worked there for seven and eight years respectively. Mr Deakin had only good things to say about them as employees; he liked the brothers very much and said that they 'bore good characters'.[43] When John first asked if Frank could come over from Ireland and work at the nursery, Mr Deakin had no concerns. 'If he is like you,' Deakin said, 'let him come.'[44] It was known that they sent money home to their parents in Ireland on a regular basis.[45] Apart from the incident with Constable Cock, and another a year earlier when John was prosecuted for drunkenness, the Habrons had not had any other dealings with the law.[46]

There was also the problem that Superintendent Bent's developing version of events seemed to overlook the fact that Constable Cock was well acquainted with the Habrons and yet, when he was asked a number of times that night who had shot him, he said that he did not know. The constable had a face to face encounter with his attacker, but was unable to identify the culprit as one of the Habron brothers. Perhaps that could be put down to the fact that it was dark at the time, or he was suffering from the effects of shock; or was it because Constable Cock had never seen his attacker before that night?

In the end the authorities ruled that Frank Habron had no case to answer regarding the murder of the constable and he was released. However, 23-year-old John Habron and 18-year-old William Habron were charged with the murder of PC 1015 Nicholas Cock and the steps were put in motion to put them on trial for the crime.

3

The Trial of the Habrons

John and William Habron appeared before Mr Justice Lindley at the Manchester Assizes on 27 November 1876. They were charged with 'feloniously, wilfully, and of their malice aforethought killing and murdering' Constable Cock. The prosecution was led by Mr William H. Higgin QC and the Habrons' defence by Mr John H.P. Leresche QC.

Mr Higgin, in his opening speech for the prosecution, went through the various facts that pointed to the brothers' guilt. He explained how close in proximity and easily accessible from the Habrons' place of work and abode was the murder scene. He referred to the well-publicised animosity that had existed between the Habrons and the victim. 'The deceased constable was distinguished,' he said, 'for the zeal with which he endeavoured to do his duty, and so had incurred the hostility of the three brothers.'[47] He explained how, because of Cock's police work, two of the Habrons had been summoned to appear in court and William had been fined. Because of this, he told the jury, the Habrons had made serious threats against the life and well-being of Constable Cock. He asserted that those threats had been carried out on the night in question. Mr Higgin then outlined for the jury the events as they had occurred on the night.

The prosecution first called a number of witnesses to collaborate the claim, made by the police, that the Habrons had made verbal threats against Constable Cock. Abraham Wilcox, a watchmaker from Chorlton-cum-Hardy, testified that when he returned a repaired watch to John Habron at Deakin's Nursery, the accused had made comments to him regarding Constable Cock. 'If he does anything to me or either of my brothers,' John had told him, 'by God I'll shoot him.' Wilcox was of the opinion that John Habron was sober when he made the threat and, in his opinion, 'spoke very earnestly'.[48] Wilcox said that he was so concerned that he told both Cock and the constable's mother about the threat.

Eleanor Carter, wife of the landlord of the Royal Oak where the Habrons were regular drinkers, made similar claims. She gave testimony regarding a number of conversations that had taken place between her and the Habrons in the weeks prior to the murder, during which they had threatened to get revenge on Constable Cock. According to Mrs Carter, John Habron, in particular, spoke 'with bitter feeling' about the constable.[49] '… if he does summons us,' she quoted John as saying, 'by God we'll make it hot for him, we'll shunt the bugger.'[50] 'Dam and bugger the bobby,' she heard William say, 'and, if he gets the day, by God, we'll finish him, and we will see an end to that bugger.'[51] By the words 'shunt' him and 'see an end' to him, it is possible that they only meant to have him transferred to another area. They had expressed that idea to a number of local people and they believed that their employer, Mr Deakin, had the power to get it done.

James Brownhill, who was employed as a wheelwright, heard an even more directly violent threat being made against Constable Cock by one of the Habron brothers. He testified that John had said to him if he was fined because of Cock '… he would shoot the bugger'.[52] Brownhill said that he did not take the comment too seriously at the time, thinking that it was just idle talk and John Habron meant nothing by it. Anyway, Brownhill knew that Cock's attitude to policing was engendering unrest and hostility amongst many of the local people; he said that the constable was regarded by the locals as being 'too forward', by which he meant too eager to prosecute for minor offences.[53] It seems that there were more than just the Habrons who would have been happy to see him sent elsewhere.

Witnesses Sarah Beck Fox and Cock's girlfriend, Elizabeth Whitelegg, also alleged that John Habron had made threats against the constable. They told of an encounter during which John said that if he was successfully prosecuted because of the constable, he would 'do him before next Wednesday'.[54]

This all sounded very incriminating for the Habrons. It must have been clear to the jury that verbal public threats had indeed been made by the Habrons against the physical well-being of Constable Cock. Whether these threats were real or just bravado on the part of the young brothers was the question that they would have to answer. Also, were such sentiments commonly expressed amongst the locals with respect to Constable Cock? It was common knowledge that many people were annoyed by the constable's conscientious attitude to his work; but that does not mean that they killed him.

Witnesses were called to testify regarding the events as they had occurred on the night of the murder. These included John Massey Simpson who, the jury heard, had been with Cock and Beanland that night and had actually seen the mysterious man believed to be the murderer. He explained how he had parted way with the constables as they went off to follow the suspicious man and two or three minutes later he heard the gunshots. He ran back and saw Beanland standing there beside Cock, whistling for help. He also saw the two workmen on their horse carts. He told of how he was confronted with the shocking sight of his friend, Constable Cock, lying seriously injured on the ground. 'Cock was lying on the footpath,' he said, '… bleeding from the breast.'[55] He told the jury how they had lifted Cock up onto one of horse carts and transported him to Dr Dill's surgery. Massey Simpson was not very convincing, however, when asked about his efforts at Old Trafford Police Station to identify William Habron as the suspicious man in the pot hat that he had seen that night:

> I did not recognise his face. The coat in colour and shape appeared to be the same as the one I saw worn by the man on the night of the murder. The man in the police office was William Habron, and was of the same height and build as the man I saw the night before. I did not particularly notice his walk. I thought the man I saw under the lamp was an elderly man from his stoop and general appearance.[56]

When Constable Beanland gave his version of events his evidence accorded with John Massey Simpson's in most respects, except that he thought Massey Simpson had left them before they ever saw the suspicious man. He seemed only a little more certain regarding the identification of William Habron as the murderer:

> I noticed that the man was young and fresh complexioned. I could see very well from the light of the gas. He was about 5 feet 7 or 8 inches in height, and dressed in dark clothes. I can't say who it was. I think now it was William.[57]

So, not even Constable Beanland could swear absolutely that the man they had seen that night was one of the Habron brothers. Under cross-examination, his doubt became even greater. 'I do not swear that the prisoner William is the same man I saw that night,' he said.[58]

Another local man called Nathaniel Williams also testified that he too had caught sight of a man prowling around on the night of the murder. It was around 'five or ten minutes to twelve at night', he said.[59] The man he saw was standing still near the gate to a local farm. Williams was unable to identify him. He also met Constable Cock walking, a few moments later, in the company of another man who he now knew to be John Massey Simpson.

The various witnesses who came to the scene of the wounded constable that night were called to give evidence. The two workmen who had arrived with their horses and carts, Ellison and Morrell, outlined the events as they had occurred from their point of view. William West told the jury how he had come on the scene and witnessed the victim lying on the ground. He said that once Cock had been lifted up onto the horse cart, he went home. Constable William Ewen said that he was 600 yards away when he heard the first shot and he ran to the scene. He confirmed, under cross-examination, that when he asked Cock who had shot him the young constable replied that he did not know. He told the court that all he said was, 'They have done for me this time'.[60]

Sergeant Moses Thompson and Dr John Dill were also called to give evidence. The doctor confirmed that 'the deceased had died from the effect of the gunshot wound'.[61] The bullet that the doctor had retrieved from the constable's body was produced in court. Sergeant Thompson confirmed what had been said earlier about Constable Cock being unable to tell them who had shot him that night, despite being asked on a number of occasions. The main plank of the prosecution case was to come next in the form of the evidence provided by Superintendent James Bent.

4

Peacefully Disposed

When Superintendent Bent took the witness stand he explained, in response to questions, that he got to Dr Dill's house just before Constable Cock had died. He told the court how he went with his men that same night to arrest the Habron brothers. He described getting the men out of their beds and having them get dressed. He repeated the comment that had been made by John Habron that night about being in bed at the time the crime was committed, even though the suspect had not been told at what time the crime had actually taken place.

One of the most important aspects of Superintendent Bent's evidence concerned the footprint that he claimed to have found in the soil near the crime scene. The superintendent was adamant that the print was a perfect match for William Habron's left boot. He gave detailed evidence regarding the nails in the sole of the boot, including the number of rows, the number of nails in each row and an irregularity to be seen in one particular row of nails. He pointed to the fact that the outside row of nails were placed close together. There were, he said, two nails near the toe and an iron plate at the toe. The heel, he told the jury, had four small nails in it. He was adamant. 'There was no single particular,' he said, 'in which the impression did not correspond with the boot.'[62]

There was a problem with this evidence, however. Although William's boot was produced as evidence in court, Superintendent Bent was forced to admit that he had not made any casts of the print in the ground, nor had any photographs taken of it prior to it being obliterated by the rain. This meant that the gentlemen of the jury would have to rely solely on the word of those who had seen the print, primarily Superintendent Bent and his men. The prosecution recalled Sergeant Thompson to the witness stand and he confirmed everything that the superintendent had said about the footprint, as did Police Inspector Thomas Whillan.[63] Police Constable

John Gillanders also concurred, along with a number of other police constables who testified in a similar manner. There was one witness who was not a constable, Mr Alfred Love, the landlord of Lloyd's Hotel, who came forward to testify that he too was present when the boot was compared to the print in the ground and he agreed with Superintendent Bent's opinion as to their similarity.[64]

It was clear from the evidence given by Mr Deakin that he was now fully convinced that his employees had nothing at all to do with the murder of Constable Cock. He told the jury that he had 'a very good opinion' of the Habrons and he insisted that they were 'peacefully disposed' men.[65] He explained how they had been working hard all that day in muddy soil, which accounted for the state of their boots. He said that the waistcoat, inside the pocket of which were found the percussion caps, had been his: he had given a number of his old waistcoats to John Habron. The caps, he thought, were most likely his as well. 'I used to carry caps in my waistcoat pockets,' he said. 'It is quite possible that some caps might have been in them when I gave them away.'[66] According to him the brothers were not allowed access to 'any caps, powder, bullets, or firearms'.[67] He was quite sure, he told the jury, that they would have had no way of getting such items on his farm. 'I kept the box with the caps locked up in a desk,' he told the court. 'There was no means of the prisoners getting to the desk.'[68]

When asked about the claim that William might have gone somewhere to buy ammunition and a revolver, he testified that the whereabouts of his employees during work time were always accounted for. He said that on the day of the crime William was busy with his work at the nursery all day. 'If any of my men had been away that afternoon,' he said, 'I must have found it out.' Superintendent Bent was not happy to hear Deakin's evidence and regarded it as a complete 'about-turn'. He claimed it differed greatly from what Deakin had said to him on the night of the arrest, 'It is somewhat remarkable to state that the gentleman who had at first told me that William Habron was one of the most abominable tempered fellows he ever knew, began afterwards to paint him as one of the most innocent creatures that ever walked'.[69]

John Walsh, who was a labourer like the Habrons, testified that he had called to the outhouse where they lived on the night of the murder to get the brothers to come out with him for a drink. 'At nine o'clock I saw Frank in bed,' he said, and 'William had his boots off'. William did not want to go out that night at all, but Walsh said that he 'pressed him' and, eventually, he agreed to go. Walsh, John and William went to Lloyd's Hotel 'before nine'. Walsh said that he left Lloyd's Hotel with them both at 'ten o'clock or after'.[70]

Henry Hayson, another labourer, saw them at the hotel that night. 'I saw John and William Habron at Lloyd's in the evening,' he told the court. 'They left about half-past ten.'[71] Ann Cabers, who was a waitress at Lloyd's Hotel, said that she also remembered seeing them. 'The prisoners were there about ten,' she said, 'and left at ten thirty.'[72] There was no evidence of them being inebriated on the night; according to Ms Cabers they only had two glasses of beer and, perhaps, John had drunk two whiskies earlier. Of course, being seen at the hotel that night meant that John and William were out and about and in close proximity to the crime scene. It might sound plausible to the jury that they had not gone straight home, but had waited around instead for a chance to carry out their threats against Constable Cock.

Other witnesses gave evidence of someone heard running that night in a direction the Habrons could have taken to get home. The implication was that this was the murderer making his escape. Mary Brundrett said that she heard running sounds between twelve o'clock and one o'clock that night on a private lane at the back of her house. Her husband got up to have a look, but did not see anything. She could not really be sure that it was not a horse or a cow. An 11-year-old boy called Edward Blakeley testified that he was staying at the house of a Mr Chambers that night, near which there was a path. He heard Mr Chambers' dog barking at 12.15 a.m. He remembered the time, he said, because the clock stuck immediately afterwards.[73]

Donald McClelland, the shop assistant at the ironmongers, was called to give an account of the man who had visited him shortly before the murder to make inquiries about buying cartridges and a revolver. The witness was still not sure if it happened on 31 July or 1 August, but he was sure that it was between 2.30 p.m. and 5 p.m., but nearer to 5 p.m. He told the court how he showed the man 'Eley's patent central-fire cartridges, No. 450, for revolvers' and a revolver designed to take that particular ammunition. He explained how Superintendent Bent came to the shop to see him after the constable's murder and asked if he would come to the station to take a look at a suspect. McClelland was asked in court directly whether he now knew the identity of his customer that day and his reply was unambiguous. 'I am sure William is the man,' he said, 'I saw his face and his dress. He had an Irish accent.'[74] He told how, although the young man left the shop that day without having bought anything, he later believed that three cartridges had been stolen from the box that he had shown him.

The problem for the prosecution was that the missing cartridges were not of the same size as the one that killed Constable Cock. There was another problem with McClelland's evidence. Also called to testify was John Henry Simpson, a fellow shop assistant who was present in the shop at the same time and who also saw the customer in question. He was not sure at first, but was now happy to say that it happened on the afternoon of 1 August, between 3 p.m. and 5 p.m. However, he said that he could still not be sure about the identification of the man. 'I cannot positively swear to the prisoner,' he said, 'but I think William is he.'[75] Of course, despite a thorough search of the Habron brothers' lodgings and everywhere near it, Superintendent Bent had to concede that 'no pistol could ever be found …'[76]

William Griffiths, a gunsmith based at Bridge Street, Manchester, with forty years' experience in the trade, was called as an expert witness. His evidence did not help the prosecution. He gave his professional opinion on the bullet that had become lodged fatally in Constable Cock's body. Outlining the technical details regarding the bullet, the cartridge of which it was part and the weapon from which it would have been fired, he said that the bullet was not the same as the ones stolen from the box produced in court by Mr McClelland; it was a size smaller. According to Mr Griffiths, the cartridge used in the murder would not fit the revolver referred to by Mr McClelland in his evidence either. As for the percussion caps found in the waistcoat pocket at the Habrons' lodgings, he simply said that the ammunition in question was a cartridge and 'caps are not wanted to fire cartridges'.[77] Therefore, Mr Griffiths' evidence about the caps rendered them virtually irrelevant to the investigation of this particular crime. Mr Griffiths testified that another cartridge, which had been found on the mantelpiece at the Habrons' outhouse, was also of a different type and, therefore, not relevant.

Day Two

The trial of William and John Habron ran over onto Tuesday, 28 November 1876, and it was on the second day that the witnesses for the defence were called. Some were called to give evidence regarding the normality of the prisoners' activities in the hours leading up to Constable Cock's killing. Those who knew them well were able to describe the characters and past behaviour of the Habron brothers in a positive light. William Kelsall, a fellow employee of Mr Deakin's nursery, testified as to the brothers' whereabouts and activities in the hours leading up to the murder and, according to him, William was working at the nursery all afternoon on that day.

If this was true, it meant that he could not have been the Irish man who visited the ironmongers that afternoon to ask about ammunition and guns. Kelsall also vouched for the characters of the brothers and their state of mind at the time. Apart from John attending court with his other brother, Frank, that day, Kelsall said that there was nothing unusual. As to their characters, '[They] have borne good characters and are peaceable men. I never heard them threaten any one.'[78] He had never heard them make any threats against Constable Cock. On the day of the murder their mood was good, as far as he could see, and there was no hint of them being angry. 'In fact,' Kelsall said, 'they seemed very jovial.'

John Cosgrove testified that he worked with William Habron in the field until eight on the evening of the murder. Again this would suggest that William was not the man who spoke with Mr McClelland about the cartridges and the revolver. Cosgrove also said that there was nothing unusual to report in either the activities or the mood of the Habrons on that day.

A controversy arose in court about what Cosgrove had said in an earlier statement to Police Inspector Henderson. Mr Higgin, in his cross-examination for the prosecution, put it to the witness that in his statement to Inspector Henderson he had said that he remembered picking raspberries on Monday, 31 July, but not much about Tuesday, 1 August, the actual day of the murder:

'Do you know Inspector Henderson?'

'Yes.'

'Did he make any Inquiries from you on this matter?'

'He did.'

'Did he write in a book what you said?'

'Yes, sir.'

'Did he read it over to you?'

'Yes, sir.'

'Did you put your mark [pointing to the book]?'

'Yes, sir.'

'Is what you told him true?'

'Yes, sir.'

'Don't mutter to yourself. If you have anything to say speak out.'

'I have nothing to say but what I said before.'

'Then what you told Mr Henderson is true?'

'Yes, sir.'[79]

It seemed from the inspector's notes that Henderson had signed a different version of events from the one that he was now giving in court. In Henderson's version he seemed much more unsure about events. Higgin read from the policeman's notebook: 'On Monday, before the murder, I, Frank, and John were getting raspberries, but I cannot remember where or how we were working on Monday or Tuesday as to time.'[80]

The interaction between the two men in court then continued:

'Is that your mark?' [Showing Mr Cosgrove the notebook]

'Yes, but it is wrong; there is a mistake in the day.'

'There is a mistake in the day? Now I understand. What days do you substitute for them? What days were you referring to?'

'Well, I cannot say.'

'I thought so.'

When Mr Leresche got his chance to re-examine his witness on behalf of the defence, he managed to get the now rattled and confused Cosgrove to clarify his statement. Mr Cosgrove's position was that on Monday he was not at work in Deakin's at all because he was ill. He said that his comments referred to Tuesday, 1 August, the day of the night on which the murder was committed and the day on which it was now thought the Irishman was asking about ammunition and a gun at the ironmongers. 'You say on Monday you were away,' Leresche asked him, 'and on Tuesday you were there?'

'Yes,' Cosgrove replied.[81]

There was controversy too regarding the evidence given by another witness and the notes taken by Inspector Henderson of his interview with her.[82] Winifred Foy was also a worker at Deakin's Nursery and she testified that William was at work all day on Tuesday, 1 August. But then Mr Higgin, in his cross-examination, referred to her statement as recorded in Inspector Henderson's notebook, which made no reference at all to the Tuesday. This seemed to puzzle the witness. 'Did you tell him anything you were doing on the Tuesday?'

'Yes.'

'Did you tell him what you have told us today?'

'I told him as near as I could guess as I have told you today ...'

'Did you tell him you could not tell him anything about the Tuesday?'

'No, Sir ...'

'What did you tell him?'

'I said I had been with William on Tuesday.'

'Did he write it down?'

'Yes.'

'Did he ask you to make your mark?'

'He did.'[83]

However, as Mr Higgin pointed out to Miss Foy, the problem was that there was nothing in Henderson's notebook about that Tuesday. Listeners were divided on the question of whether these two witnesses had decided to change their stories and lied in court in order to help their co-workers, or if Inspector Henderson had failed, either by accident or design, to make an accurate report of what they had said to him.

A number of other witnesses from Mr Deakin's farm also gave evidence testifying to the normality of the day spent by the Habrons prior to the alleged shooting of the constable that night. If one was to believe their co-workers the brothers seemed calm and happy on that day, not agitated, angry or nervous in any way. Nothing was reported either in their activities or mood that would suggest their involvement in a heinous crime a few hours later. As to the question of William Habron being able to sneak off, unnoticed, to buy ammunition on the afternoon of Monday, 31 July or Tuesday, 1 August, their statements, if true, seemed to make this almost impossible as he was accounted for at work during those times. The question for the jury was whether these witnesses were actually telling the truth, or lying to support their co-workers.

William Raines, a local physician, and John Gresty, a market gardener, testified to the prisoners' characters, describing them using the words 'peaceable', 'well-conducted', 'decent' and 'quiet'. Raines said that he had known them 'familiarly' for 'five or six years'.[84] Whether the jury would regard any of this evidence about their characters as proof of anything was, as yet, unknown.

6

Closing Statements

Once all the witnesses for both sides had been heard, it was time for the legal teams to make their closing statements directly to the jury. Mr Leresche began his speech for the defence by telling the jury members that it was 'his duty to put before them views likely to assist them in reference to this most important issue they had to discharge'.[85] He acknowledged that a terrible crime had taken place, '... the policeman was on his beat, going his accustomed rounds at midnight, when he was shot dead, and that not by accident, but by a deadly weapon used by a person who knew what he was doing'.[86]

That was not at issue. He also understood, he told them, that the people of Chorlton and Whalley Range were 'very much disquieted by this incident'. That only made it more '... imperative ... that they should have the most cogent, conclusive, irresistible evidence before they brought the crime home to any prisoner. It was a case in which they could come to no compromise.'[87] Although everyone accepted that a terrible and immoral crime had been committed by someone, he argued that there was no reason at all to believe that either of the Habron brothers were guilty of that crime. With regard to his clients, he said, it 'was either murder or it was nothing at all'.

Before they could return a verdict of guilty, the jury members would have to be satisfied that the prosecution had proven the case against his clients. 'The question was, was there any evidence ... which brought home conclusively and affirmatively to their minds that the two men the prosecution had put in the dock were guilty of the crime with which they were charged?'[88] There was, he asserted, no credible evidence for such a conclusion. On the contrary, in fact, 'there was an entire absence of direct evidence in this case'.[89] The prosecution case was built on evidence that was entirely circumstantial and this, according to Leresche, would not do for such an important case. A jury, he told them, could not rely on circumstantial evidence because such reliance had been found wanting in the past:

> ... it was a matter which the history of the law (particularly the criminal law) had shown to be surrounded with difficulties, and accompanied also in many cases by the gravest uncertainty ... it was a class of evidence which required careful watching. There should not only be a continuous chain, but each individual link in it must be perfect.[90]

Leresche urged the gentlemen of the jury to consider only the facts of the case. If they did so, he told them, the Habron brothers would be 'entitled to leave that Court freed from that terrible charge'.[91] He reminded them that there had been only one witness to what had actually taken place that night and that was Constable Cock himself, but when the constable was asked repeatedly about the identity of his attacker he had been unable to give one.

He asked them to consider what possible motive could have driven these young men to commit such a terrible crime? Why, Leresche asked, would they have 'such a deadly malignant feeling as to induce them to shoot the policeman dead?'[92] The motive of revenge, as had been proposed by the prosecution, did not make sense. It was just not credible. The threats that the Habrons were alleged to have made against Constable Cock, he argued, were nothing more than idle talk:

> ... nothing more than the rash, coarse way of speaking, too prevalent amongst the lower classes, which any observant person in passing down the street had heard over and over again. However violent the language used, they must not attach too much importance to what were, after all, mere breath and random expressions.[93]

There was, he argued, 'nothing to induce them to come to the horrible determination to shoot a fellow-creature'. 'Surely,' Leresche said, 'the flimsy pretext suggested was not a sufficient motive.'[94]

Leresche addressed the question of the boots and the print found on the ground at the crime scene. Firstly, it was irrelevant that William's boots were muddy, or 'slutchy' as they had been described by Superintendent Bent. There were 'plenty of muddy pools, which would account for the state of his boots,' he said.[95] His job, after all, meant that he was working out in the fields all day. As for the print allegedly made by William's boot at the crime scene, he dismissed this print as evidence. He said that the prosecution had only managed to produce one footprint from the scene of the crime, which they claimed to be a match for William's boot.

They did not even have a pair. Furthermore, no reproduction of that print could be produced in court for comparison with the actual boot.

Then there was the question of the murder weapon. It had not been found. Leresche pointed to the fact that the authorities had never been able to show that any of these men had ever even possessed a weapon such as the one used in the murder of Constable Cock:

> This was not a case where a long period having elapsed between the committal of the murder and its discovery, there would have been an opportunity to remove all traces; but it was a case where, within a few minutes after the man was shot down, the superintendent arrested the suspected men, when they could not have had any time to make away with any weapons. If anything had been thrown away, it must have been found. The police had emptied every ditch, turned over the silt and mud, dug up the fields, and found nothing.[96]

The fact that the weapon had not been found by a policeman as 'zealous and intelligent' as Mr Bent was an important fact in this case, according to Leresche. 'It was,' he argued, 'presumptive evidence of the accused's innocence that after all this searching nothing was found.'[97]

It was nonsense, according to Leresche, to claim that William Habron was the man who called on Mr McClelland and showed an interest in buying ammunition and a revolver. He asserted that McClelland was simply mistaken about the identity of the man. Even his co-worker, Mr Simpson, had been unable to positively identify the man in question as William Habron. None of William's co-workers believed that he could have sneaked off to buy ammunition and a weapon during working hours without them noticing his absence from the nursery.

As to the controversy that had arisen in court about the evidence of Mr Cosgrove and Miss Foy and Inspector Henderson's notes, all Leresche had to say was that Inspector Henderson 'might be a good police officer, but he was a very indifferent note-taker'.[98]

All in all, Leresche claimed, the prosecution was relying on evidence that was wholly circumstantial and inadequate. A jury must, he told them, 'reject any link in the evidence which was faulty'.[99] Considering all this, he told them that they were left with only one option. 'Taking all the evidence into consideration, the only course which they as fellow-citizens could pursue in this momentous case was to find the prisoners "not guilty".'[100]

Mr Higgin, in his closing statement on behalf of the prosecution, told the jury that he had no fears about the veracity of the charge being brought against these prisoners and had no worry about the evidence being labelled as 'circumstantial' by his colleague, Mr Leresche:

… circumstantial evidence might be as strong, as powerful, and as convincing as the most direct evidence. It might as strong as if they saw the act committed, … and therefore presuming that he was addressing men who were desirous of approaching the case from a reasonable and sensible point of view, he believed they would not be frightened by being told it was a case of circumstantial evidence.[101]

Higgin reassured the gentlemen of the jury that they were not required to convict someone based on one single piece of evidence and neither was it a requirement that they be convinced about every single piece of evidence. He asked them 'to consider those particular points which were proved to their satisfaction, to dismiss those which were not so proved, and then to put them all together and ask themselves, as sensible and reasonable men, what conclusion they pointed to'.[102]

Contrary to what Mr Leresche had said, Higgin urged the jury to believe the evidence that had been given by the shop worker at the ironmonger's, Mr McClelland. That evidence proved that William Habron was intent on buying cartridges immediately prior to the murder of Constable Cock. It was very significant that Mr McClelland was quite happy to testify that the customer that day was William Habron, while his fellow shop worker 'had a confident belief' that it was him.[103] The defence had tried to dismiss Mr McClelland's evidence, but Higgin said that it was much more credible than anything said in court by the co-workers of the accused men. Two of them, as far as he was concerned, 'were proved to have come here to say that which they knew to be untrue'.[104] He was, of course, referring to Cosgrove and Foy, whose testimony had contradicted Inspector Henderson's notes.

Higgin dismissed the idea being put forward by the defence that the Habron brothers were peace-loving citizens who would not injure or kill anyone:

… they were said to be peaceable and quiet men. If that were so, they indulged in the strangest possible language, and carried in their breasts the most deadly and savage revenge. It did not seem … that quiet and decent persons should be going about to public houses using such threats as had been stated, and that they should, if they believed the case for the prosecution, be shooting down a policeman in the dark.[105]

He told the jury members that 'if they could say with safe consciences that these men were innocent of the crime laid to their charge no man in that Court would rejoice more than he'.[106] But what if:

… about twelve o'clock on this particular night, the prisoner, William, was near the place where the deceased was shot, in company with his brother, John, who that very morning had uttered threats against the deceased, and if afterwards William was found under suspicious circumstances in the place where he slept …?[107]

Higgin told the gentlemen of the jury that the only reasonable conclusion they could reach was that William Habron 'was the man who fired the shots' that night. His only desire was, he told them, that there 'be no failure of justice' in this case.

In Accordance with Human Nature

Mr Justice Lindley made it clear from the beginning of his final statement to the jury that he viewed the Habron trial as having great importance:

> … this particular murder was that of a policeman on his beat; and not in the course of a struggle or in the course of any riot or disturbance. It was done, so far as one knew, without any immediate provocation, and it was therefore, in the highest degree desirable, and in the highest degree important, in the interests of the public that the person who killed that policeman should be found, and … brought to justice.[108]

He realised that the killing of Constable Cock had got considerable attention in the newspapers and was a topic of conversation amongst the public, especially since it had occurred 'in one of the most respectable suburbs' and 'at so short a distance from the town'. Consequently, he acknowledged, the jury members had probably heard a lot more about the case outside of the courtroom than he had.

Justice Lindley reminded them that their duty was 'to find out the truth if they could' and not to rely on what they had heard or read.[109] In one way it was very simple, he told them, 'Did the prisoners, or either of them, shoot this man Cock?'[110] He broke the issue down into two main questions. Firstly, was it a fact that Cock was murdered? On this question, Justice Lindley felt that there was little doubt, 'It had hardly been suggested that he came by his death in any other way. But, apart from that, they could, by attending to the evidence, come to the conclusion that he must have been murdered.'[111] He was, after all, killed by the bullet that had been extracted from his body and 'there was not the slightest reason to suppose that the deceased inflicted it himself'. Neither was there any evidence of an accident or a struggle having taken place, so, Lindley concluded, 'Whoever did the deed must have done it deliberately, and with a desire to take the man's life'.[112] They could be confident that it was a case of murder.

The second question, he told them, was 'much more difficult and serious'.[113] Was it the Habron brothers, one or both of them, who murdered Constable Cock? The Habrons had been heard 'to utter threats against the deceased' and so 'it was in accordance with human nature that they … should be suspected of murdering him'. Nevertheless, Lindley warned the jury members that it was their duty to distinguish between 'reasonable certainty' and mere 'suspicion'. They would have to work out whether the evidence was 'consistent with the guilt of these men' and 'fairly inconsistent with their innocence'.[114] Only if they were satisfied about this should they return a verdict of guilty on one or both of the prisoners.[115]

The justice then dealt with some matters concerning the evidence. On the question of whether William Habron had asked about buying ammunition and a gun from Mr McClelland shortly before the murder, he told the jury that 'it was a very important fact if it could be satisfactorily established …'[116] After some initial doubt, he said, it seemed to be established that the customer in question had come into the ironmongers on the Tuesday of that week, which was 1 August and only hours before the murder.

They would have to satisfy themselves as to the question of the man's identity. Was it William Habron? There was uncertainty about it. Mr McClelland said it was him, while his co-worker could not swear that it was. The testimony given by the workers from Deakin's Nursery suggested that William Habron did not go anywhere during working hours on that Tuesday. The justice made special reference to the evidence of Mr Cosgrove on the matter and how the man had given a different account in court from the one that he had given to Inspector Henderson earlier. Justice Lindley said that he found the man's evidence 'very unsatisfactory' and said that it 'must be taken with caution, not to say with suspicion'.[117]

What about the other workers from Deakin's? His opinion about Cosgrove did not suggest that they were all lying. If they were all telling lies about William Habron being present at the nursery that afternoon, he said, it meant that they had all been 'banded together to speak an untruth'.[118] That was something, according to Justice Lindley, that the jury members would have to satisfy themselves about.

As for the boot print found at the scene of the crime, Justice Lindley told them that as they had no copy or impression of the boot in question, they would have to rely mainly on the testimony given by Superintendent Bent. Of course, in that case they would have to be assured that the witness was 'desirous of telling the truth' and 'probably they would be fully satisfied on that head'.[119] If that was so, then their next concern would be 'was he possessed of habits of accurate observation, not merely of general appearances, but of minute particulars?'[120]

There was a problem:

Boots, especially those worn by labouring men, were made in great numbers, and were more or less like each other. Anyone who would say that any impression was made by any particular boot, unless they could show some particularly defined features in the boot, was not worthy of belief.[121]

Of course Superintendent Bent had pointed to a number of 'particularly defined features' of the boot in question. As they did not have an impression of the print before them, they would have to decide whether to depend on the superintendent's testimony as to the similarity of the print in the ground with the particular features of William Habron's left boot. The superintendent, he reminded them, had referred to a number of details concerning nails and 'irregularly arranged' rows and so on. 'These,' the justice said, 'were the sort of things that one would look to in order to distinguish the impression of this boot from that of other boots.'[122]

'How far have you got?' he asked the gentlemen of the jury at one point. 'Did either of the prisoners shoot the deceased?' He turned to the evidence against each defendant in turn. Firstly John: no one was claiming that the suspicious man seen in the vicinity of the crime scene that night was John Habron. There was some uncertainty about the time that he actually went to bed on the night in question and there was that comment that he had made to Superintendent Bent about being 'in bed at the time' of the crime when no precise time had been mentioned. The justice asked the jury to consider whether there was enough evidence to convict him on any one of three grounds: '… first, of shooting the deceased; second, of aiding and abetting; third, of previously inciting and urging men to do it.'[123]

As for William Habron, there was, he said, the evidence given by John Massey Simpson and Constable Beanland 'such as it was'.[124] Then, of course, there was the footprint. If you are of the opinion, he told them, that the print 'was not that of William' you will have 'but little difficulty in dealing with the case. If, on the other hand, you believe that the print was produced by William's boot, the question becomes "when it was made?"'[125]

Justice Lindley reminded the gentlemen of the jury that it was their duty to consider carefully the evidence that had been produced in the prisoners' favour. Despite what the court had heard about their relations with Constable Cock, he reminded them that a number of people had testified that the brothers 'were of good character'.[126] There was also the point that 'when arrested they were where they ought to have been – in bed'.[127] One other important point in their favour was that 'no trace of firearms had been found'.[128]

At five minutes to five the gentlemen of the jury retired to consider the matter. After a deliberation of the facts for two and a half hours, they returned with a verdict: John Habron was found not guilty, while his brother, 18-year-old William Habron, was found guilty. The jury made a recommendation of mercy in William's case, in recognition of his tender age. When Justice Lindley asked William if he had anything to say as to 'why sentence of death should not be passed upon him', his only reply was, 'I am innocent'.[129]

Notwithstanding the plea from the jury for mercy, Mr Justice Lindley then donned the black cap and proceeded to pass sentence upon William:

> You have been found guilty by the jury of having murdered Police Constable Nicholas Cock. It is my duty to pass sentence upon you. The trial has been long, but not unnecessarily so, for the evidence which had to be adduced against you consisted of a number of small details which had to be proved, and all of which had to be carefully considered together. The jury most patiently attended to the whole, and they found the verdict they have just found. I shall simply discharge my duty by passing sentence of death upon you. It will be my duty to present to Her Majesty's Government the recommendation to mercy which the jury have made by reason of your youth; but having regard to the fact that they have found you guilty, you must not be deceived – for this murder, which is now found to have been a murder committed by yourself, was a cruel murder – and you must not be surprised if that recommendation is disregarded. However, that does not rest with me, but with Her Majesty's Government.[130]

As he was taken down, William Habron raised his hand into the air as a sign of his exasperation and quietly repeated the words, 'I am innocent'.[131]

As one young man was led away to a terrible punishment, public shock and grief at what had happened to another young man was reflected in the inscription carved on the memorial stone erected at the grave of Constable Cock. It described him as 'An Able and Energetic Officer of the County Constabulary who ... was cruelly assassinated'. It said that he was 'for zeal and fidelity in his office ... worthy of honoured remembrance by all'.[132]

Superintendent Bent was still not content with the outcome. He was unhappy that John Habron remained free. He was fervently of the opinion that John was as capable of violence as his brother and just as guilty of Cock's murder. Even after his acquittal, Bent issued John with a stern warning, telling him that 'if any person who had given evidence in the case received any injury' he would hold him personally responsible and 'would find him if he went to the other end of the world ...'[133] Nevertheless, for now at least, the case of Constable Cock's murder was closed.

A small man had sat in court for the past two days, mostly unnoticed except by those sitting near him who said that he had demonstrated considerable specialist knowledge of the law by imparting pertinent facts throughout the trial. It was obvious that he was engrossed in the proceedings. This man's interest in the trial was not passing or incidental, and he would later have a significant bearing upon its aftermath.

Part 2

The Banner Cross Murder

Around eight o'clock on 29 November 1876 a small man stood in the bright moonlight watching the home of Arthur and Katherine Dyson at Banner Cross, Sheffield. The day before he had been at the court in Manchester to see William Habron sentenced to death for the murder of Constable Cock. The man, sporting a long white beard, was dressed almost completely in black, apart from the touch of white running between the dark stripes on his necktie.

The Dysons had only moved to Banner Cross recently but were settling in well and were liked by their new neighbours. They had spent a considerable length of time in the United States of America. Arthur Dyson was a very tall and thin man, who stood 6ft 6in. So tall was he, in fact, that an especially high desk had to be provided for his comfort at work. He was described, variously, as being a 'genteel' man, 'not too robust of health', 'big, but delicate'. His wife, Katherine, thought by many to be an American, actually came from Maynooth in Ireland. She had emigrated to America, at the age of just 15, to join her sister in Cleveland, Ohio. It was in America that she first met her British husband. Katherine Dyson was regarded as a very glamorous woman by the people of Sheffield and described as a buxom, blooming 25-year-old with dark hair. The couple had one son.

Arthur Dyson was a civil engineer by profession and had decided to return from America in the early 1870s in order to take up a position with the North Eastern Railway Company. He came home to England having gained valuable experience working for the Atlantic and Great Western Railway in America. One of his jobs had been as superintendent engineer on the construction of a railway bridge across the Mississippi River.[1]

The Dysons settled in Yorkshire, living firstly with Arthur's mother in Tinsley, from where they moved to Highfield and later to Healey.[2] They eventually moved into a house in Darnall, on the outskirts of Sheffield, a decision that Katherine would later regard as a fateful one, saying, '... it was there that my troubles began'.[3] These 'troubles' were the reason that they had moved to Banner Cross and also why the bearded man in black was now standing outside their house.

The stranger was standing in a passageway to the rear of the Dysons' house. He made no effort to keep out of sight and, earlier, had called into Gregory's grocery shop, located right beside the Dysons' house, where he asked to see Mr Gregory.

The husband and wife team, John and Mary Ann Gregory, ran the corner shop together. Mrs Gregory had seen this man once before, about a month earlier, when he was hanging around the area and had bought some tobacco from her husband. She informed him, on this occasion, that her husband was not at home but was expected any minute.[4] In truth, she was not sure when her husband would be home and only said that because, for some reason, she found this 'short and slightly built man' to be intimidating.[5] Five minutes after the man had left the shop, Mrs Gregory looked out of the front door and saw him 'creeping down [the street] as slowly and quietly as possible, as if he did not wish to be seen'.[6]

The stranger also had an encounter on the street with a woman called Sarah Colgreaves. Mrs Colgreaves was on her way to Gregory's shop when the man approached her, pointed to a house, and asked whether she knew the people who lived there. He was pointing to the Dysons' house. She told him that she did not know them. He then asked her if she knew that they were strangers and she replied that she did. 'You don't know them then?' he said, and she told him again that she did not. 'That woman is a bloody whore,' he then said.

'You ought to mind what you say,' a rather shocked Mrs Colgreaves told him, now anxious to get away from him. He asked her to deliver a message to the Dysons' house. He said that he wanted her to tell the woman of the house that there was a gentleman outside to see her. Not surprisingly, Mrs Colgreaves refused to deliver the message.[7] 'Go yourself,' she told him, walking away. When she got to Gregory's shop, she told Mrs Gregory about the man she had just encountered on the street. She asked Mrs Gregory to lock the door and, since the shopkeeper's wife was feeling just as anxious about the stranger's presence, she was pleased to oblige.[8]

Charles Brassington was standing in front of the Banner Cross Hotel that night, which was located quite near both the Dysons' house and Gregory's shop. Brassington, a labourer from Ecclesall, first noticed the man in black 'walking backwards and forwards on the causeway'.[9] Having walked past Brassington a number of times, the man then spoke to him. 'Have you seen some strangers who have come to live in this neighbourhood?' he asked.[10] Brassington told him that he did not know them, but the man insisted on showing him some photographs and letters under the light of the street lamp. The man mumbled a comment about them being 'a nuisance to the country'.[11] Brassington told him that he was unable to read the letters. The man then made a chilling comment. 'I'll make it warm for the strangers before morning,' he said, 'I'll shoot them both.'[12] The last sight Brassington got of him, the man was walking off in the direction of the Dysons' house.

The man stood outside the simple two storey, terraced house, and could see Mrs Dyson inside moving around an upstairs bedroom with a candle in her hand, putting her 5-year-old son to bed. Mr Dyson was reading downstairs. Once the child had settled down for the night, Mrs Dyson came outside and walked down the passageway that ran beside the terrace of houses and led to a backyard. She was on her way to the water closet. Mrs Gregory heard the familiar sound of her neighbour's clogs as she walked down the laneway past their shop. Shortly afterwards, Mrs Gregory heard Mrs Dyson scream loudly and she ran to her back door. She saw Mr Dyson, standing at his own back door, and she called out to him, 'You had better go to your wife, Mr Dyson!'[13]

Arthur Dyson rushed off towards the yard. Shortly afterwards two shots rang out and Mrs Gregory, although she had gone back inside her shop and locked the door by this time, heard the shots clearly, followed by another scream. She then heard the clattering sound of rapid footsteps going past the shop.

The stranger had fired two shots at Mr Dyson from close range. The first bullet missed and lodged in the stone wall; the second hit Mr Dyson in the temple causing him to collapse instantly on his back. Katherine Dyson ran to her husband and cradled him in her arms. She shouted at the man who had just committed this awful deed, 'Murder! You villain! You've shot my husband.'

Leaving the heavily bleeding Arthur Dyson in the arms of his weeping wife, the man ran down the passageway and out onto the road. He hesitated there for a moment, not sure what to do next, before crossing the road and climbing over a wall.[14] He could not help but hear Mrs Dyson's cries for help in the background as he did so. Thomas Wilson, a young 17-year-old scythe maker from Brincliffe Hill, was standing on the road at the time and saw the figure of the man running away. He could not see the man clearly and would not be able to identify him again if he saw him. The murderer had got away.

Meanwhile, neighbours began arriving in response to the sound of the gunshots and Katherine Dyson's chilling screams for help. They included Thomas Wilson and Mrs Gregory. When he saw the scene, Wilson ran to fetch a doctor. The wounded Arthur Dyson was carried into his house by neighbours; he was unable to respond to them. They tried to stem the bleeding from his head. Mr James William Harrison, the surgeon who arrived to attend to Mr Dyson, found him unconscious and bleeding profusely from a wound in his temple. The neighbours had propped him up in a sitting position. 'He was in a chair. There was a lot of blood about his feet and on the floor. He seemed to bleed from the left temple, and he was unconscious. I had him laid down on the floor and attended to him.'[15]

Mr Dyson died in his own house about two hours later. The surgeon carried out a post-mortem examination shortly after death and reported that he found a bullet lodged in the left lobe of Mr Dyson's brain, 'running upwards and backwards'.[16]

When the police arrived, Mrs Dyson was able to give them the identity of her husband's murderer. She said that the man was well known to her. He had been their former neighbour at another address, with whom they had been having trouble for months. His name, she said, was Charles Peace. That was a name well known to the constables – Charles Peace was one of the country's most prolific and skilled burglars.

The murder of Arthur Dyson, however, was not the result of a burglary gone wrong; it was a case of love thwarted.

9

Humble Beginnings

Charles Frederick Peace was born on 14 May 1832, at Nursery Street in Sheffield. His father, John Peace, lost his left leg as a result of an accident suffered while working as a collier at Burton. He was forced to support his family for a time by becoming a trainer of wild animals at a travelling show known as Wombwell's Wild Beast Show. He trained Peace's older brother in the art of working with wild and dangerous animals, but after the child died, probably from smallpox, he was so distraught from the loss that he decided to leave the show.[17] After that he worked at a number of jobs including that of a shoemaker. Peace's mother came from more lofty heritage in Hull, being the daughter of a respected naval surgeon. Charles Peace had a surviving brother called Daniel and a sister, Mary Ann.

At the age of 14, with his schooling over, Charles Peace started working at a local steel rolling mill in Sheffield. It was hard and dangerous work. A tragic event, reminiscent of his father's experience, occurred while he was working there one day and it may well have changed the course of his life. He was operating one of the many dangerous machines at the mill when a mishap occurred and a hot steel rod shot right through his leg. Unlike in his father's case, Charles' limb was saved, but not without a lot of pain and over a year spent in the infirmary at Sheffield. He walked with a slight limp for the rest of his life. At a time when an able body was virtually essential for the survival of a boy from a working-class background, Peace would thereafter be forced to find a more unconventional way of making a living.

Whatever Peace may have lost in physical attributes, he was abundantly endowed with ability and personality. While employed at the rolling mill he was popular with his fellow workers who enjoyed, in particular, his party piece of throwing a heavy ball of shot into the air and catching it in a leather pouch attached to his forehead. He also displayed ample proficiency in storytelling and acting, and was said to be able to recite from memory a number of Shakespearean soliloquies. He was skilled in the arts of taming wild cats, no doubt a skill inherited from his father, and paper model making.

He became an accomplished musician, teaching himself to play the violin using an instrument with only one string and he performed in amateur theatrical shows using his stage name, 'The Modern Paganini'. As with most things in Peace's life, his approach to music had a strong element of the novel or downright bizarre about it; not content with playing on a single-stringed violin, he also liked to produce music using a poker. His method involved fixing a strong string across a room and tying onto it a large poker, known as a 'potter'. He would then hit the poker with a stick and amaze his audience by playing on it, in this way, a selection of popular folk tunes. It was a feat he liked to perform in public houses late at night after an evening spent drinking.

Peace's unusual musical talents did not end there. Detective Parrock, of the Staffordshire police force, remembered him playing music using his teeth in a most unorthodox manner:

> By a curious twist of his elastic mouth he would bring his jaws into a peculiar form, incidentally disclosing a very full and perfect set of teeth. Then, laying back … he would bring out a succession of distinct and harmonious notes by striking his teeth with the fingers of either hand … In this manner I have heard him play such difficult selections as those from *Faust* and *Il Trovatore* through from beginning to end, and never once could I detect a mistake or false note.[18]

The detective also witnessed him making music on a string held between his teeth. As well as music, Peace adisplayed talent in painting, design and the making of ornaments. The renowned painter William Frith commented, much later, that Peace's work possessed 'the true feeling of an artist'.[19] A prison warder who was familiar with Peace also remembered his artistic endeavours: 'He was fond of cutting out of a rough kind of cardboard a variety of objects – birds, beasts, fishes, horses, and the like. The Royal Arms was a favourite subject with him, and when paints were available he would colour his productions.'[20]

Had things in his life worked out differently, perhaps the name Charles Peace would have become notable in the world of the arts or entertainment rather than crime. It was, however, to crime that Peace turned in order to make a living. Around the time that he was still trying to recover from the terrible injury to his leg, his father died at the age of 64. The added financial pressure on Peace brought forth the less constructive side of his personality.

He was still only a teenager when he committed his first crime, stealing a gold watch from an elderly gentleman in his locality. From then on he began to develop the skills of the professional burglar and, it is safe to assume, had committed many crimes before his first encounter with the law on 26 October 1851, at 19 years of age.

Peace was caught in possession of property that had been stolen from a house at Mount View in Sheffield. Although arrested and convicted of the crime, probably due to a favourable character reference from his former employer at the mill he got off lightly, receiving only a month's imprisonment. This relatively short sentence may have been Peace's final opportunity to turn away from crime and create for himself an honest future instead. As one writer puts it, 'twas a sorry offence, which merited no more than a month, so that he returned to freedom and his fiddle with his character unbesmirched.'[21]

It was not, however, an opportunity of which he took advantage. On release from prison he resumed his criminal ways and three years later, in 1854, was in trouble with the law again. An amount of property, mostly jewellery, had been stolen from a number of homes in the Sheffield area and some of the items taken from the house of Mr Richard Stuart at Brincliffe Edge were discovered by police in the possession of Peace's sister, now called Mrs Mary Ann Neil, and a girl with whom he was having a relationship at the time, Emma James. All three of them were arrested and charged.

At Doncaster Sessions on 20 October 1854, Peace was sentenced to four years' penal servitude, while both women were imprisoned for six months. His sister, Mary Ann, died soon afterwards. This latest debacle showed that Peace was still inexperienced in the ways of crime: he did not have a trusted 'fence' to whom he could pass the stolen goods, nor did he have a secure place to store the booty. In order to hide it he solicited the assistance of amateurs and, worst of all, family members.

While serving a stint at Wakefield Prison, Peace decided to attempt an escape. According to one version of events, he managed to ingratiate himself with the prison staff to the extent that he was allowed to undertake some minor repair work around the prison. This enabled him to smuggle a ladder into his cell. Then, using a saw made of tin, he cut a hole in the ceiling of his cell through which he was able to gain access to the roof of the building.

It was a stroke of bad luck that, just as he was exiting through the hole, a prisoner warder happened to come into his cell. Peace knocked the man to the ground and made his way onto the roof, aware that the alarm would soon be raised. As he ran along the high wall of the prison as quickly as he could, a number of loose bricks caused him to fall off, unfortunately for him, on the prison side. Still undeterred and uninjured, he made his way to the governor's house. He slipped inside and, finding the house empty, treated himself to a hot bath and changed into the governor's clothes. He laid low there for an hour and a half, hoping things would quieten down and he would get an opportunity to escape.

In the end that opportunity never arose and he was captured in the governor's bedroom. Peace was placed in solitary confinement as punishment. This may have affected him deeply as there are reports that he tried to commit suicide by inflicting 'a very severe gash in his throat', causing a scar which remained afterwards.[22]

Peace managed to serve out the rest of his sentence quietly and, towards the end of the 1850s with this second period of detention behind him, he married a widow called Hannah Ward at St George's Church, Sheffield. Hannah had a son, Willie, from her first marriage and soon gave birth to Peace's daughter, who was given the name Jane Ann.

The fact that Peace now had a wife and family did not cause him to abandon his criminal activities and, before long, he was back in trouble with the law once again. On 11 August 1859, he broke into the house of a Mrs Elizabeth Brooks at South Villa, Victoria Park, Rusholme, in Manchester, and made off with a considerable haul of valuables which he then stashed away in a hole in a field near Brighton Grove. Unfortunately for him, the police discovered his hiding place and put it under twenty-four hour surveillance. When Peace arrived to reclaim his goods, he was set upon by the waiting constables.

Not wanting to return to prison, he fought hard not to be arrested and nearly killed one of the policemen in the process. He then tried unsuccessfully to convince the constables that his name was George Parker and he was a music professor from Nottingham. This time, despite the fact that he convinced his mother to come to court and swear that he had been with her on the night of the robbery, he was sentenced to six years' incarceration. A very poor start to married life, you might think, but then one presumes that Hannah knew what she was getting into from the beginning.

10

Going Straight

Released from prison in 1864, Charles Peace returned not only to his family but also to his criminal activities. Despite his bad leg he was gifted with a natural agility and this skill along with his small size, only 5ft 4in tall, was of great advantage to him as a burglar.

On one particular occasion, when interrupted in his 'work' by the owner of the house, he is said to have hidden himself by curling his body around the single leg of the dining table, clear of the ground and hidden by the tablecloth. According to the story, he remained there motionless until the man of the house went back to bed. With experience, his 'skills' as a burglar seem to have been improving and this time he managed to avoid arrest for two years.

In 1866, however, his lucky streak came to an end when he was caught 'red-handed' in the act of burglarising a house in Lower Broughton, Manchester. On this occasion he was arrested easily and without putting up much of a fight, a fact he later put down to having consumed a large amount of whisky and being drunk at the time. At Manchester Assizes on 3 December 1866 Peace was sentenced to seven years in prison.

Peace served prison time at both Millbank and Gibraltar and also at Chatham, where he was flogged for his part in a riot. It was reported that while he was incarcerated at Gibraltar a fellow prisoner, who was known to have crossed him, went missing and was found dead at the bottom of a cliff. The officials were never able to prove if the man's death had been the result of an accident or something else.

In 1872 Peace was granted his freedom a little early under a ticket of leave and returned to Hannah and the children in Sheffield. It seems he had decided that it would be wise to start acting as a law-abiding, normal citizen. Hannah opened a reputable eating house at 37 Collier Street in Hull and Peace himself set himself up in business as a picture framer. It looked, on the surface, as if he was finally ready to settle down and end his criminal activities.

To someone who did not know Peace's criminal history, the family would have appeared utterly respectable. They attended religious services regularly and the children were sent to Sunday school. Peace even took to carving beautiful wooden images of the saints. He was also utilising his abilities in the field of entertainment. There is an account of a dramatic performance given by him in a school around this time:

> It is a curious fact that in about 1873 or so, while I was a boy at school in Highgate, this rascal came, and, with permission of the headmaster, gave a recitation in the Big School to us boys, and chose the grave-digger's scene from 'Hamlet'. We had, in consequence, nearly a half-holiday, and much enjoyed it.[23]

The truth, though, was that Peace still believed that crime was his best way of making a comfortable living for himself and his family and he was soon back to his illegal night-time endeavours. At some point he lost a finger, or more than one according to some reports, perhaps shot off during one of his many dangerous escapades. To hide such a distinguishing feature, not a good thing for a burglar, he chose the rather bizarre option of wearing a homemade false limb, which he constructed out of gutta-percha, with a hole down the middle into which he placed his arm. At the end of this device was a steel plate with a hook attached. He became so adept in using the hook that he was able to perform many dextrous feats with it, including using it to pull himself up onto a tree or a portico roof in order to gain entry to a property. It meant that any potential witnesses might describe him, inaccurately, as a man with one arm rather than a man with fingers missing.

There is a story told of a robbery committed by him in Sheffield in November 1874, which demonstrates his degree of imagination and invention.[24] He had been watching a jewellery shop for some time to assess its level of defence against burglary. From his surveillance he became aware that a junior member of staff usually slept on the premises, most probably with an armed revolver at his side, and a very unfriendly bulldog was kept in the backyard. He knew that in order to pull off this job he would have to gain more specific information than he could glean from distant observation alone.

With this in mind, he cleaned himself up, donned his best suit and walked into the shop brandishing a business card which identified him as a sales representative of a London firm that supplied office furniture. He managed to get a meeting with the boss, during which he convinced the man that he was there to tell him about an exciting new invention called the electric burglar alarm. With the very concept of electricity being such a new one, it is no wonder that the jeweller had never heard of such a thing. When the man declared himself very satisfied with his present security arrangements, Peace got him to elaborate on what they entailed. Not only that, but Peace inveigled a tour of the premises out of him, during which the man pointed out the various precautions they had taken. Peace left the jewellery shop that day with an order for the installation of a new electric burglar alarm system.

As the story goes, Peace returned to the shop after closing time, scaled the back wall easily and dropped calmly into the back yard. He had no need to worry about the ferocious bulldog as the animal was lying unconscious at his feet having consumed the drugged meat that he had first dropped over the wall. Having been alerted to their presence, he was able to deal easily with the shop's other security measures, including the bell that was attached to the door by a virtually invisible length of wire. As neither Peace, the dog nor the bell made any sound, the armed junior member of staff continued to sleep soundly throughout. Peace filled his pockets and bag with a variety of goods from the shop and left as easily as he had arrived.

The jeweller, in the aftermath of the robbery, was annoyed that his new alarm system had not yet been installed and wrote to the office furniture company to complain about the fact. The following slightly bewildered reply came from the company:

Dear Sirs, – We have received yours of the 17th inst. duly to hand, but beg to say your complaint leaves us completely in the dark as to its cause …

In the matter of electric alarms, which you mention, we would point out we have no such line catalogued amongst our other items of office furniture, nor were we even conversant with the fact that it was proposed to use electricity in any such way.

Further, our traveller has not called on you to the best of our knowledge since last march, though we have now given him special instructions to do so when next in Sheffield. – We are, yours, &c.[25]

This, for Charles Peace, may have been a most satisfying robbery, but events in his life would soon take a more deadly turn.

A Demon Beyond the Power of even a Shakespeare

It was late in 1875 that Peace and his family moved to one in a row of cottages on Britannia Road in a suburb of Sheffield called Darnall. This is when he first met Arthur and Katherine Dyson, who were his neighbours of one door away.

When the Dysons had decided to leave America and move back to Arthur's homeland, it was only natural that they were hopeful for a happy future. It was clear, however, that Katherine had loved America. She was a woman with great energy and zest for adventure, as was obvious whenever she spoke of her life in America:

> The life had … many charms for me. I am a good hand at driving and am fond of horses … I always used to drive Mr. Dyson. He used often to say that I could drive better than he, and he would sit back in the buggy while I held the reins and sent the horses along. I liked the excitement of driving him to and from his work and especially when we were in new country and he was out surveying. I have driven him through forests where there were bears and over creeks swollen by floods. The horses often had to swim. I remember on one occasion sending the horses and the buggy over a river and then coming over myself on a piece of timber.[26]

Life in Darnall was very different and no doubt Katherine soon grew bored. Then Arthur lost his engineering job with the railway.

The arrival of Charles Peace, the picture framer, to Darnall would only make matters worse. Before long, it seems that the bored Katherine Dyson was having a relationship of some kind with the exciting but dangerous Charles Peace. The exact extent or nature of that relationship would be contested by both parties later.

Peace claimed it was a close, intimate one and Katherine denied it was anything such. They were, according to her, nothing but friendly neighbours:

> You will naturally ask how I became acquainted with Peace. It was impossible to avoid becoming acquainted with him. Besides, at that time I did not know the sort of man he really was. He lived next door but one to us at Darnall, and he used generally to speak to Mr. Dyson on going in and out. Mr. Dyson was a gentleman, and, of course, when Peace spoke to him he used to reply.[27]

Peace, according to Katherine, was continually trying to engage the Dysons in conversation, even using his pet birds to lure them. 'One of his favourite means was to place his parrots and his other birds upon a wall. He could then call our attention to them, and to what they could do, and thus get us into conversation with him.'[28] He even started playing with the Dysons' little boy and bringing him with him, in order to ingratiate himself with the family.

At first they were not too concerned about Peace, Katherine said, as he seemed like a 'nice old man' and was 'plausibility itself'. He even got Arthur Dyson to write out his receipts for his picture framing business because, as the Dysons thought, he could not write very well himself. However, over time, Peace's interactions with them became more and more intrusive. 'Peace wasn't content with a merely speaking acquaintance,' Katherine said later. 'He wanted to force himself upon us.'[29]

Much of the evidence does not seem to support Katherine's claim of a purely platonic and neighbourly friendship between herself and Peace. For a time they seemed to be quite close. There is considerable evidence to suggest that they began to spend a lot of time together without the presence of Mr Dyson. If they were not at Peace's house, they were on nights out at the music hall, or drinking together in public houses such as the Marquis of Waterford. They were photographed together at the Summer Fair in Sheffield as a charming couple; Peace dressed in his tall hat, frock coat and gloves, leaning over the back of the chair on which the resplendent Katherine sat.

In addition, there is evidence that Katherine and Arthur Dyson's marriage was not always as harmonious as Katherine would later try to claim. There were at least 'one or two occasions' when the police had been forced to intervene in their fights and make peace between them. 'Mr Dyson has practised the art of throwing at his wife, and she in turn has wielded the poker at him, with very marked effect.'[30]

A correspondent of the *New York Times* may have later described Peace in that photograph taken at the Summer Fair as looking 'like a respectable mechanic in his Sunday clothes' but, of course, there was nothing respectable about Charles Peace. That would soon become very clear to the Dysons. Katherine herself described the dawning realisation:

Mr. Dyson soon began to tire of him. My husband had travelled, and could converse on many subjects. Peace was plausible enough, but his language was not good; in fact, he very soon began to show that he was anything but a gentleman. Mr. Dyson could not stand that, and Peace showed him some obscene pictures, and my husband said that he didn't like a man of that kind, and wouldn't have anything to do with him. Besides, another thing greatly repelled Mr. Dyson. It was this. Peace wanted to take him to Sheffield to show him what he called the 'sights of the town'. Mr. Dyson knew what that meant, and being, as I have said, a gentleman, he became much disgusted at Peace.[31]

Perhaps the truth is that by this time Arthur Dyson had also become aware of Peace's relationship with his wife. In any event, by 1876 Peace's personal relationship with Katherine had gone sour and she now wanted nothing more to do with him. In fact, she is reputed to have said that she came to regard him as a demon 'beyond the power of even a Shakespeare to paint'.[32]

The problem was that she could not get rid of him. The obsessive Charles Peace refused to accept her change of mind. He could not accept that their relationship was over and he began to harass the Dysons, even watching them through the windows of their house in the evenings. By now Katherine obviously had some insight into Peace's personality and she became very afraid of him:

When he found that he could no longer gain access to the house, Peace became awfully impudent. He would, for instance, stand on the doorstep and listen through the keyhole to what we were talking about, or look through the window at us … he would come and stand outside the window at night and look in, leering all the while; and he would come across you at all turns and leer in your face in a manner that was very frightful.[33]

He had a way of creeping and crawling about, and of coming upon you suddenly unawares; and I cannot describe to you how he seemed to wriggle himself inside the door, or the terrible expression on his face. He seemed more like an evil spirit than a man.[34]

Katherine knew what his ultimate aim was. 'His object was to obtain power over me, and, having done that, to make me an accomplice of his … he wanted me to leave my husband! Positively to leave my husband.'[35] Peace even told her that if they went away together, he would set her up in business:

If you will only go to Manchester … I will take a store … for you, and will spend £50 in fitting it up. You shall have a cigar store, or a picture store.[36]

You are a fine-looking woman. You will look well in fine things, and I will send you fine clothes and jewellery … If you will only do what I want there shall not be such another lady in England as you may be … You will have a splendid business, and will live like a lady.[37]

Although Peace was offering her all these wonderful things, Katherine was not impressed by the way he was treating his own family. Peace's wife, she said, would 'go out every morning washing bottles' to make money.[38] They seemed to her to be poor. On one particular occasion when Peace offered to buy Katherine 'a sealskin jacket and several yards of silk', she claimed to have told him that 'if he had a sealskin jacket and some silk to spare he had better make a present of them to his wife and daughter'.[39]

Katherine knew that Peace would not be a man to give up easily. He had told her so on many occasions. 'If I make up my mind to a thing,' she remembered him saying, 'I am bound to have it, even if it cost me my life.'[40]

In June 1876, Arthur Dyson felt that he had to take some action about Peace's continual harassment of them. His rather tame action came in the form of a card thrown into Peace's garden on which were written the words 'Charles Peace is requested not to interfere with my family'. Of course this very modest and polite attempt to warn him off was not sufficient to deter someone like Charles Peace. On the contrary, it seemed to only inflame matters further.

On 1 July 1876, Peace saw Dyson walking in the street and he came up behind him and tried to trip him up. The incident was seen by a neighbour, Rose Annie Sykes, who was looking out of her window at the time. Later that evening, Mrs Sykes and her husband were chatting on the street with Katherine Dyson and two other friends, Mrs Padmore and Mrs England, when Peace approached them. Undeterred by the presence of the witnesses, he threatened to blow both Katherine and her husband's brains out. In order to emphasise the point, he then pulled out a pistol and held it only 6in away from the terrified Katherine's face. He addressed Mr Sykes, saying, 'Jim, you are a witness that she struck me with a life preserver.'[41] The others did not know what he was talking about as they had never seen Katherine strike anyone.

'No,' said Mr Sykes, 'I am a witness that you pointed a pistol at her head, and threatened to blow out her brains.'

As he walked off, Peace looked back at them. 'I have got enough ammunition here,' he said, 'to do for half of a dozen of you.'

The Dysons now felt that the situation was getting very dangerous and it was necessary for them to seek legal protection against Peace. They contacted the police and a summons was issued against him. However, when the case came to be heard in court, Peace failed to appear and a warrant had to be issued for his arrest. Peace had suddenly disappeared from Darnall. He had, in fact, moved his family to Hull.

This did not prevent him from still trying to intimidate the Dysons. Letters began to arrive from him, or written by someone on his behalf. The correspondence was addressed as if it was being sent from Hamburg in Germany, but Katherine did not believe that he was out of the country. She knew that it was just another one of his clever tricks. The letters, she said, threatened her not to give evidence against him.

Fearing that Peace might return at any time, Arthur and Katherine Dyson decided that their best option now might be to move to a new address altogether and get safely away from his intimidation. So, on 26 October 1876 they moved quietly to another suburb of Sheffield called Banner Cross, in the hope that the whole episode with Charles Peace could be put behind them.

Katherine, however, was shocked when one of the first people she saw in their new neighbourhood was Charles Peace. Even worse was the fact that he was coming out of the door of their new home, while their belongings were only just being moved in. Peace was in the company of his son-in-law, William Bolsover, at the time. 'You see,' Peace shouted at her with glee, 'I am here to annoy you, and I'll annoy you wherever you go.'[42] Katherine reminded him that there was a warrant out for his arrest, but he replied that he did not care about either the warrant or the police.

Later on, Peace, still in the company of Mr Bolsover, passed Arthur Dyson in the street and tried to intimidate him by producing a revolver from his pocket and saying loudly, 'If he offers to come near me, I'll make him stand back'.

During his visit to Gregory's shop that evening Peace bought half an ounce of tobacco and engaged John Gregory in conversation. He told Mr Gregory that he had some advice to give him about his new neighbours, the Dysons. 'They are very bad people,' he said, 'they will get into debt if they can and will not pay you.'[43] He said that he would send Mr Gregory some letters to prove it. The Gregorys never received any letters from him.

That Night in Banner Cross

On 29 November 1876, the conflict between Charles Peace and the Dysons reached its deadly conclusion. Just the day before, Peace had been a spectator at the court in Manchester where the young William Habron was sentenced to death for the murder of Constable Cock. He had attended the court specially and had, it seems, found the whole spectacle highly entertaining. There is some indication to suggest, from his behaviour, that he may have arrived at Darnall that night in an intoxicated state. He had been seen earlier in a public house in Ecclesall in a highly celebratory mood, entertaining the customers by performing his party trick of making music from a poker.

Not surprisingly, the stories told by Katherine Dyson and Charles Peace about what actually happened on the night of Arthur Dyson's shooting diverge in the detail. According to her, she came out of the house to use the water closet at the back of the yard, leaving her husband inside reading. She was carrying a small lighted lantern. On leaving the closet, she was confronted by Peace.

Peace's version of events is somewhat different. He said that she came out willingly to meet him. 'I watched her for some time, cracked my finger, and gave a low whistle to attract Mrs Dyson's attention, as I had often done before at other places. Mrs Dyson came downstairs. She knew the signal, and in response to it she came out.'[44]

Peace claimed that he was only there to discuss the possibility of having the legal summons that the Dysons had placed on him revoked. In both versions of events Peace then pointed his revolver at Mrs Dyson. Peace claimed that he did so only because she was 'very noisy and used fearful language and threats'.[45] She claimed that she did not speak to him at all and, in fact, he said to her, 'Speak, or I'll fire'.[46] It was then that Mrs Dyson screamed and shut herself back inside the water closet.

It was that scream that Mrs Gregory heard from her shop before running to her back door and calling out for Mr Dyson to go and see if his wife was all right.[47]

Arthur Dyson made his way towards the back yard to see what was going on. When she heard him approach, according to Katherine's account, she came out of the water closet once again. Mr Dyson was now confronted with the sight of his wife being held at gunpoint by Charles Peace. According to Peace, he then made for the passageway that ran along the side of the house in order to get away from the jealous husband but, he claimed, fury had got the better of Arthur Dyson and he came after him in an aggressive manner. According to Peace the two men then became involved in a violent life and death struggle in the passageway, during which his pistol went off killing Arthur Dyson accidently.

Katherine claimed that this was not a true account of what had happened; she said that no physical struggle had taken place between the two men. Her husband did walk down the passageway after Peace, but did not get near enough to grab him or for a struggle to take place. In her version, when Peace got near the end of the passageway he just turned and fired his revolver at Mr Dyson, '… he turned round and faced my husband and fired'.[48] Luckily, that first shot hit the wall. Then Peace fired a second shot. This time Arthur Dyson was hit in the temple and fell instantly to the ground on his back.

When the police constables arrived at the scene Katherine Dyson gave them Peace's name and description and informed them about the history of the events that had led up to this. Charles Peace would always claim that Arthur Dyson's death had been a complete accident. But, whether that was true or not, he was now Britain's most wanted murder suspect.

The police may soon have begun to question the nature of Katherine Dyson's relationship with Charles Peace. Inspector Jacob Bradbury had been shown, in his chief constable's office, the photograph of Katherine and Peace together at Sheffield Fair. This suspicion was compounded when Police Constable George Ward's search of Mrs Else's field across the road from the crime scene turned up some very interesting documents that seem to have been dropped by the murderer. There were also some footprints in the ground a few yards from the documents and an American cent coin inside an envelope marked 'C. Peace Esq.'

The documents consisted mostly of short handwritten notes rolled up together, but not tied. Constable Ward handed the documents and the coin up to Inspector Bradbury. Amongst the documents was the card that Mr Dyson had thrown into Peace's garden requesting that Peace leave them alone. Most of the others, over twenty separate pieces of correspondence, consisted of short notes allegedly sent by Katherine to Peace.

If these notes were indeed dropped by Peace that night, one might ask why he was carrying them around with him? Was it just another aspect of his obsessional attachment to Katherine that he had them on him? Indeed, it soon emerged that he had been showing them around the neighbourhood in public houses and other places as proof of his relationship with Katherine. He had even visited the vicar at Banner Cross on a number of occasions, including just hours before the murder, with 'what he called his proof of the grave allegations he had previously made'.[49] Perhaps he was planning to show the notes to Arthur Dyson that night as well in order to drive a permanent wedge between the couple. Katherine's contention was that Peace had painstakingly forged these documents in order to fabricate a close relationship between them. Peace's aim, she said, was to cause a rift between herself and Arthur by inventing things that were untrue.

Many of the notes did seem to show that a close friendship, at the very least, had existed between Katherine and Peace. They made interesting reading.[50] In the middle of comments about framing jobs that Peace was undertaking for the Dysons, there were many personal comments. If the notes are to be believed, at one time Katherine found her relationship with Peace to be very positive for her. She is very appreciative about the support and help that Peace was giving her. 'I write you these few lines,' she says in one note, 'to thank you for all your kindness, which I shall never forget.' Another note says, 'Many thanks for your kind advice. I hope I shall benefit by it. I shall try to do right by everyone if I can, and shall always look upon you as a friend.'

The notes also show, however, that Katherine had a lot of regard for Peace's wife and family as she mentions them favourably a number of times. If the notes are forgeries one would wonder why Peace would include such comments as these. She sends her love frequently to his daughter, Jane, and obviously holds his family in high regard. In one note she thanks Peace and his wife for their kindness and she makes a comment about Hannah, 'She is a very good one'. In another she says, 'I will thank your wife as soon as I have a chance to see her for her kind present. Tell her so with my love.'

Katherine, or at least the author of these notes, even comments on a row that she heard going on between Peace and Hannah. 'I was very sorry to hear your quarrelling,' she writes. 'Hope it is all settled now … you have a good wife. Be kind to her.' The Katherine in the notes is concerned about her and worried that she might get hurt. 'Does she know you are to give me the things or not?' she asks Peace at one point. 'How can you keep them concealed?' Another says, 'You can give me something as a keepsake if you like, but I don't want to be covetous and take them from your wife and daughter. Love to all.'

The notes contain many references to covert meetings having taken place between Katherine and Peace and much scheming going on behind Arthur Dyson's back. 'After he is going out I won't go if I can help it,' she writes, 'So see me.' In another she says, 'I will write you a note when I can, perhaps tomorrow.' Such comments continue throughout the notes:

I don't know what train we shall go by for I have a good deal to do this morning.

Will see you as soon as I possibly can. I think it will be easier after you move. He won't watch so.

I will tell you what I thought of when I see you about arranging matters.

If you have a note for me, send now while he is out, but you must not venture for he is watching and you can't be too careful ... He went to Sheffield yesterday, but I could not see you anywhere. Were you out?

This was written yesterday, but could not see you.

He won't say when he is going. Not today anyhow, he is not very well. I will write to you when I have a chance ...

Don't know when he will go out again but will sure tell you.

The use of the expression 'will sure tell you', which is American in syntactical construction, led some people at the time to believe that Katherine must have written that note at least.[51] But then, of course, the question is would Peace be clever enough to mimic Katherine's way of speaking, if he was forging the note, to make it seem more authentic? The incriminating comments continue:

He only went for tobacco and he has not been out. I shall tell you when he does.

I think I will go by nine o'clock now. You must not go by train. Go by tram because he will go down with me. Don't let him see anything of you. Meet me in the Wicker. Hope nothing will turn up to prevent it.

Be quick – you – he is out now.

A number of the notes suggest that Katherine was very worried that her husband would find out about the relationship with Peace. If they are to be believed, she seems, at one point, to be more afraid of Arthur than of Peace especially when, as the notes suggest, he did find out: 'Things are very bad,' she writes, 'for people told him everything. Do keep quiet, and don't let anyone see you.'

Katherine shows her annoyance in some of the notes that Peace is not trying hard enough to hide their relationship and is, in fact, talking openly about it. 'It looks as if you want people to know ... If you are not more careful we will have to say quits. I have told you not to say anything.' In another place she warns him:

You are getting very thick with old Ned; don't blab anything to him for it will be all over. Never speak of me … I will give you the wink when the coast is clear but you must not take notice till I tell you or you will make a mess of it because he is always on the lookout.

The writer of the notes asks for money on a number of occasions. One, in particular, is quite direct about this – 'Money, send me some.' Then there is also a gift of a ring. 'The r[in]g fits the little finger,' she says. 'Many thanks.' Alcohol is also mentioned: 'Will you send me a shilling or two and a drop and keep very quiet, be quick.' And on another occasion, 'Send me a drink. I am nearly dead.' At the end of some of the notes the writer tells Peace to burn them when he has read them.

The notes are another contradictory aspect to the divergent narratives that Katherine and Peace would tell about the time that they had known each other. It is very difficult for anyone to determine where the full truth lies.

The notes became an issue at the official inquest into the death of Arthur Dyson, which was held on 8 December 1876 at the Stag Inn, Sharrow Head, Sheffield. The inquest was presided over by the coroner, Mr Dossey Wightman, and the main witness appearing before the jury was Katherine Dyson herself. Katherine testified that Charles Peace had murdered her husband and she outlined her version of the events as they had occurred on that night. When her attention was drawn to the bundle of handwritten notes, she said that it was the first time that she had heard of them.

The coroner was unsure of how they should be dealt with. 'The difficulty, gentlemen,' he explained to the jury, 'is to know what to do with regard to these letters. They are not addressed.' He referred to one of the notes and said, '… it may have been written by Mrs Dyson or it may not have been'.[52] He turned to Katherine directly on the matter, 'Did you ever write a letter to Peace in your life?'

'No', she answered, 'I have never written to him.'

'Neither on a scrap of paper nor anything?'

'No.'

'Never wrote a word to him on paper at all, do you mean to say?'

'No.'

'Now just be careful, please. Do you mean to swear that you never wrote a word to him on paper?'

'No; I never wrote to him on paper.'

'Never a word?'

'No.'

Katherine remained adamant throughout that she had never written anything to Peace. If these notes could be proven to be authentic, of course, it would not reflect well on her. *The Times* newspaper of the following morning commented on them: 'The contents of the letters were such as a woman might write to a paramour, and most of the scraps of paper were intimations that "he" was out, and that the coast was clear.'[53]

The coroner turned from the controversial notes to the other evidence about that night. Amongst the witnesses called to give evidence at the inquest was the young scythe maker, Thomas Wilson, who heard the shots that night and saw the figure of a man running away from the scene. He would not, he said, be able to identify that man if he saw him again. He explained how, after he heard the shots, he ran to Dyson's house to see what had happened and it was he who went to fetch the surgeon, James William Harrison.

Mr Harrison was also called to give evidence at the inquest. He was now in a position to reveal more detailed information about Mr Dyson's injuries. He had conducted a thorough examination of the body with the assistance of a colleague called John Benson:

The wound on the left temple was about an inch above the external orbit of the eye, and I could pass in the little finger right though it to the skull, and into the brain. There was a quantity of effused blood between the skull and the scalp. Upon taking the scalp away from the skull, I found a circular opening in the skull about an inch in diameter. The opening went through the anterior inferior angle of the parietal bone. The ball went through the brain in a direction upwards and backwards through the left lobe, and was found lodged on the upper surface of that lobe.[54]

The direction in which the bullet had travelled led the surgeon to reach two conclusions: firstly, that 'the man who fired the shot was in a lower angle than the deceased' and, secondly, that it made it unlikely that the deceased had fired the shot himself.[55] A brother of Arthur Dyson's, who was in court, was eager to make a comment about any suggestion that Arthur could have fired the fatal shot himself:

You asked, Mr. Coroner, Whether it was possible for my brother to have shot himself? All I have to remark is, that had he done so he must have been a left-handed man according to the position of the wound in the left temple; and my brother was not a left-handed man.[56]

Other witnesses gave evidence at the inquest, including Mrs Gregory from the local shop, Mrs Colgreaves, Constable Ward and Mr Brassington.

The coroner asked Katherine if she had given the American cent coin that had been found in the field to Peace and she was adamant that she had never given him such a coin. In a sense the issues about the notes, the American coin and even whether Katherine had been engaged in some sort of illicit romantic dalliance with Peace were incidental. The important issue for the coroner and the jury was whether Charles Peace had shot and killed Arthur Dyson that night in Banner Cross.

The coroner told the jury that he found the evidence to be 'really very conclusive'.[57] He could not see, he said, how they could reach any other conclusion but 'that Peace went there, having a pistol in his possession, with the determination to shoot either one or both of the parties'.[58] The coroner's jury deliberated for only a few minutes before returning a verdict of 'wilful murder' against Charles Peace.

Life on the Run

The jury at the inquest may have come to the determination that Charles Peace should be arrested on a charge of committing the wilful murder of Arthur Dyson, but the problem lay in finding him. Immediately after the shooting, he had disappeared into the night and no one knew where he was.

In actual fact, Peace escaped to the centre of Sheffield that night, where he got a cab to the church gates. It is believed that he had a relative living near there, in Spring Street, at whose house he changed his clothes. He also paid quick visits to his brother and his mother. He now needed to utilise his considerable powers of disguise and subterfuge to evade his potential captors. He spent the next twenty-four hours moving about, quickly visiting a number of railway stations and Yorkshire towns, including Rotherham, Beverley, Normanton and York.

The day after Arthur Dyson's murder or, as the press soon began to call it, the Banner Cross murder, he walked casually and audaciously into Hannah's eating house on Collier Street in Hull. As he sat eating a meal prepared by his wife, two policemen came in and inquired whether Charles Peace was lodging with her. Peace looked on as she told them that she had not seen the rogue for two months. They informed her that they would have to conduct a search of the property. Some customers told them about a side door to the premises, which they went off to investigate. This gave Peace the chance to slip up to a back room, climb out through a window onto an adjoining roof and hide himself behind a chimneystack until the constables had gone. He was forced to do exactly the same thing later that day.

Peace's notorious infamy was spreading quickly. Wanted posters announced the reward of £100 that would be paid to anyone who provided information leading to his capture and conviction:

MURDER

One Hundred Pounds Reward.

WHEREAS on the 29th ult. Mr. … Dyson, C.E., was murdered at Banner Cross, Sheffield, having been shot in the head in the presence of his wife by Charles Peace, who escaped in the darkness of the night, and is still at large, and WHEREAS at the coroner's inquest … upon the body of the said [Arthur] Dyson, a verdict of wilful murder was found against the said Charles Peace, NOTICE is hereby given that a reward of one hundred pounds will be paid by Her Majesty's Government to any person other than a person employed in a police-office in the United Kingdom who shall give such information and evidence as will lead to the discovery and conviction of the said Charles Peace.[59]

Despite the manhunt, Peace remained in Hull for around three weeks but it was getting progressively more dangerous for him. He shaved his grey beard off, dyed his hair and took to wearing a pair of blue spectacles which, it was said, 'altered the appearance of the little, cunning, wizened-up face, and hid those ferrety eyes …'[60] He applied walnut juice to his skin to darken its tone. He made use of a unique skill that he possessed; an ability to contort his face, mostly by protruding his lower jaw in such a way as to markedly alter his appearance. *The Times* would later refer to this rather bizarre skill: 'A … singular gift was his power of facial contortion, in which he appears to have equalled some of the greatest actors, and on which he relied so confidently that he ventured to face the police … and was never detected.'

A one-time friend of Peace's told the press how surprised he and others had been at this ability:

> … he asked the spectators to turn their backs to him a bit. They did so, and on turning around were astounded to find that Peace had completely altered the expression of his face, and had so protruded his chin and curled his lips that in ordinary circumstances it would have been impossible to recognize him …[61]

Detective Parrock, who worked for the Staffordshire police force and later the Metropolitan force, knew him for years and wrote of having followed Peace one day and observed his almost instantaneous transformation from a limping, rather hunched up figure into 'a young man, upright and sprightly'.[62] It was as if the normal everyday appearance that he showed to most people, especially the police, was itself a disguise. Before his transformation Parrock had even felt sorry for him. 'He would sit all hunched up in the corner of the carriage,' he said, 'with his head, which seemed too large for his body, lopping over on to one shoulder.'[63]

Peace made use of many disguises to evade arrest. This image depicts him as a bespectacled gentleman. (Mary Evans Picture Library)

One of the simplest methods Peace employed to avoid being recognised was to dress well. 'I made a point of dressing respectably,' he said, 'as the police never think of suspecting anyone who appears in good clothes. In this way I have thrown the police off their ground many a time.'[64] It was also reported that he had been spotted dressed as a woman on a few occasions when he was stalking the Dysons.

He was always boastful about his skills at evading arrest. 'I can dodge any detective in existence,' he once claimed.[65] 'I have often met the best London detectives,' he said, 'and stared at them right in the face, but they can't recognise me.'[66]

Katherine Dyson, too, knew about this uncanny ability to change his appearance. 'He would … assume all sorts of disguises,' she said. 'He used to boast how effectually he could disguise himself.'[67] No doubt Peace read with great interest and some amusement the descriptions of himself that were being circulated by the police:

Charles Peace. Wanted for murder on the night of the 29th inst. He is thin and slightly built, from fifty-five to sixty years of age, five feet four inches or five feet high, grey (nearly white) hair, beard and whiskers. His whiskers were long when he committed the murder, but may now be cut or shaved off. He lacks one or more fingers off the left hand, walks with his legs rather wide apart, speaks somewhat peculiarly as though his tongue were too large for his mouth, and is a great boaster. He is a picture-frame maker. He occasionally cleans and repairs clocks and watches and sometimes deals in oleographs, engravings and pictures. He has been in penal servitude for burglary in Manchester. He has lived in Manchester, Salford, and Liverpool and Hull.

That the authorities were confused about his appearance was demonstrated by the fact that they were later forced to alter his description somewhat, changing his age to 46 but saying that he looked ten years older than that. He was, in fact, 44 at the time. They also added a number of aliases that were known to have been used by him such as George Parker, Alexander Mann and his stage name Paganini.

Peace knew that constantly moving around gave him the best chance of staying free, so as the year 1876 drew to a close he was doing just that. As he travelled, living a fugitive existence, he went on a burgling spree that ranged across multiple locations including York, Manchester, Doncaster, London, Bristol, Birmingham, Bath, Oxford and Derby. One particular train journey to Oxford became interesting when he found himself in the company of an unwitting sergeant of police. The sergeant failed to identify Peace as the most infamous suspect in the country, a fact about which Peace seemed quite confident. 'He seemed a smart chap,' he would say later, 'but not smart enough to know me.'

This fugitive existence and relentless travel seemed to be his best option for the present.

New Love in Nottingham

In January 1877, Charles Peace arrived in Nottingham and sought refuge in the home of Mrs Adamson, a woman he had been using for some time as a receiver of stolen goods. It was while staying there that he met the next love of his life, a woman called Susan Gray. Gray appears to have been her maiden name and she often used the name of her one-time husband Mr Bailey as well. In fact, she seems to have been happy to use any name that was convenient at a particular time. Susan's complexion and hair were fair, her eyes were brown.

Peace was aware that Sue, as he called her, had a propensity for heavy drinking and the imbibing of other questionable substances. 'You know,' he said, 'she is a dreadful woman for drink and snuff. She snuffs half an ounce a day; and as for drink, I have paid as much as £3 in two days for her.'[68] Nevertheless, once Peace had fallen for Sue, as with Katherine Dyson an obsession took hold of him and during one drinking session he threatened to shoot her if she did not become his lover. Sue, it seems, had no desire to reject his advances and they began an intimate relationship.

They started living under the assumed identities of Mr and Mrs John Thompson. They even had the audacity to lodge as a couple at the house of a police sergeant. The policeman regarded Mr Thompson as an ideal lodger, especially since in conversation he seemed to show a genuine interest in police work. Peace continued to support them through his burglary.

The risks, of course, were still extremely high. In June 1877 he was almost captured by the police while stealing some blankets and only managed to escape by brandishing his revolver.

When he felt that things had quietened down sufficiently back in Hull, he decided to return there, bringing Susan Gray with him. He continued his criminal activities in Hull and other places which, as usual, placed him in a number of very dangerous situations.

One night while busily robbing an attractive villa residence he was disturbed by two men and two women. He ran out onto the first landing of the property but was met there by a number of other people coming up the stairs. He drew his revolver and fired a shot at the ceiling, which was sufficient to cause the ladies and gentlemen to back away allowing him to made good his escape through the back garden. One brave man did pursue him, but another warning shot fired into the air was sufficient to deter him.[69] On another occasion he found a constable drunk on the beat and made sure to take advantage of the opportunity, robbing six houses in a row and stealing a particularly large amount of valuable plate from the house of Mr Ansell, a member of the town council.[70]

After a number of close escapes in Hull and surrounding areas, Peace decided that he and Sue should go back to Nottingham. Of course, a mysterious crime wave was soon perplexing the local constabulary of that city and a reward of £50 was put on the head of the perpetrator.

Peace came close to capture on one occasion when a constable, investigating a robbery, burst into a bedroom to find him in bed with Sue. Peace didn't panic:

> The officer wanted to know who I was and where I came from, and I at once replied that I was a hawker. The officer asked for my licence and what I was carrying. I told him that my licence and the goods I was carrying were down stairs and said if he would go down and wait till my wife and I got up I would show them to him.[71]

When the naive constable complied with this request, Peace, of course, used the opportunity to slip out through a 6in gap between the bars in the window and escape.[72] He told Sue to say that she knew nothing about him. Peace hid in a neighbour's house and even sent the woman from that house back for his boots. Later he sent a note to Sue telling her where to join him.

There was yet another occasion when, in order to evade the constables, he ducked into a boys' school and passed himself off as a travelling actor hoping to put on a performance.[73] The pupils spent the next few hours listening to England's most wanted man as he entertained them with his memorised Shakespearean soliloquies. He would later speak freely and proudly of the robberies he committed in and around Nottingham:

> At Nottingham I done a big tailor and draper establishment for a lot of overcoats and cloth. I think it is in Castlegate … I then done a very big mantle place in Derby for a number of women's mantels and money … I went back to Nottingham and done a great many gentlemen's houses. I then went to Melton

Mowbray to a Lord's house and brought away a great quantity of valuable jewels and plate.

There is a story associated with this robbery of the lord's house in Melton Mowbray during these years.[74] Peace managed to gain entrance to the big house without too much trouble and filled his pockets and bag with the family's precious heirlooms and valuables, which were said to be worth over £4,000. As he was climbing out of the window to make his escape, though, he found his foot alighting upon something solid, which he soon realised was a ladder, but not his own.

He could not believe it as he looked down to see the ladder set against the wall, surrounded at the bottom by a group of agitated servants. One particular hardy character was even beginning to make his way up the ladder towards him. Perturbed only for a second, Peace began his descent and met the man, a gardener, halfway between the top and bottom.

Peace was far too battle hardened a criminal for any gardener to arrest. Without any hesitation, he hit the man in the face and sent him crashing to the ground. At this act of violence there was consternation and anger amongst the man's colleagues. One of them rushed to the ladder and sent it toppling over with Peace still on it. The ladder fell, sending broken wood in all directions and Peace fell to the ground, uninjured. Two of the servants then attempted to apprehend him but were easily punched to the ground. They could only watch as the robber was about to escape from their clutches.

The servants had one final hope for his apprehension – the bloodhounds were let loose and sent in pursuit of the villain's scent. It was too late; Peace and the family valuables were gone. 'When I saw I'd bungled over the ladder business,' Peace would later comment, 'I set myself to get away with the swag or give up the trade for good and all; and I got away.'[75] It is clear from this statement that his perverse sense of professional pride would not allow him to be apprehended by a bunch of amateurs.

There is another story, about Lord Shaftesbury's salubrious house in Wandsworth, which Peace burgled twice in six weeks because, he said, he had to go back to get 'what I was unable to carry off the first time'.[76] He made several hundred pounds on that job alone.

All the while he was on the run, Peace was continuing to take a perverse pleasure in being able to outwit the authorities and his victims. He loved nothing better than to flaunt himself right in front of the police without detection. He even claimed to have done so to one of the senior officers pursuing him:

Upon one occasion I booked from Nottingham to Sheffield, but got out of the train at Heeley Station, and walked past the police station at Highfields – Inspector Bradbury stood at the police station door – at about seven o'clock at night. I passed close by him, and he did not know me …[77]

Of course the police were getting many reports about Peace's whereabouts from the public, but most were spurious. One woman was more conscientious than most. 'A respectable elderly woman in Sheffield is under the hallucination that she has a "mission from the Lord" to arrest the murderer, and in prosecuting this "mission" she has paid frequent visits to the Highfield Police Station, and has called upon the widow of the murdered man.'[78]

This lady was not the only one trying hard to assist the police:

> Another amateur detective says it was revealed to him in a dream that Peace had thrown himself down a disused shaft in Ecclesall. He saw the shaft clearly in his dream, and next day went straight to it. He did not find Peace there, but thinks the dream is an intimation to him that he is 'ordained' to apprehend the murderer.[79]

Then there were the times that the police got it wrong:

> A man, supposed to be Charles Peace, who murdered Arthur Dyson … by shooting him in the head, in the presence of his wife, and who escaped in the darkness, is supposed to be in custody at Hexham. He was destitute when apprehended, and represented himself to be Henry Le Miere. In appearance he exactly corresponds with the description given of Peace. The case is under investigation.[80]

The real Charles Peace, along with Sue, returned to Hull for a short time but found that Hannah's place was being visited by the police on a regular basis. Peace decided that it would be wiser for them to lose themselves for a while in the anonymity of a city the size of London.

A Lavish Life in London

No one was suspicious when a respectable dealer in musical instruments and his family moved into 25 Stangate, Lambeth, London. The residents could not have known that their new neighbour, Mr Thompson, was really the infamous murderer and thief, Charles Peace. By day Peace played the role of reputable musical instrument dealer, and by night he burgled the homes of the rich in Camberwell and other affluent parts of south London.

He did particularly well from one property at Denmark Hill, although the job was not without its difficulties. While scavenging downstairs he was lucky enough to come upon a safe. It was, however, proving difficult to open. Undeterred, he crept upstairs and found the owner of the house asleep in his bed. He removed a bunch of keys from the pocket of the sleeping victim's trousers, which he found lying upon the bed; he opened the safe and made off with a valuable plate collection that made him £250.[81]

There were many other successful jobs: a 'silk dress and £30 in plate' from Streatham; jewellery from Kidbrook Terrace in Blackheath; 'watches and plate' from Herne Hill.[82] Then there were the jobs further afield, such as Southampton where one robbery was said to have netted him £200 in valuables.

Peace's criminal activities during this period proved so profitable that he was soon in a position to move to Crane Court, Greenwich, and later to a pair of adjoining houses in nearby Billingsgate Street. He also had the money to furnish his new homes in a lavish style. He lived in one of the adjoining houses with Susan Gray, known to all locally as Mrs Thompson, while his wife Hannah and her son, Willie, also moved to London and took up residence in the other one. Many people were under the impression that Hannah was the maid. This unorthodox marital arrangement did not lead to domestic harmony; the two women argued a lot, due mostly to Sue's drinking habit and Hannah's understandable jealousy.

Soon, however, this unusual family was on the move again. Sue's taste for the high life was obviously intensifying and she grew tired of Greenwich. In May 1877, Peace moved his whole entourage to 5 East Terrace, Evelina Road, Peckham, where he took a plush suburban villa with a basement for £30 a year. The house was elegant both outside, with its majestic bow window and steps running up to the front door, and inside where 'the front door opened into a moderate sized hall, and a large drawing room communicated by means of folding doors with a spacious sitting room behind'.[83]

Peace cut no corners on adding to the furnishings and decorations, '... the drawing room: gorgeously furnished – a costly suite of walnut furniture, rich Turkey carpet, many mirrors, a bijou piano, a Spanish guitar, said to have been looted from a countess'.[84] The drawing room suite was said to be worth 60 guineas and the Spanish guitar, with its elaborate inlay much admired by guests, had an estimated value of 30 guineas.[85] Of course, it is no stretch of the imagination to assume that the items in question had been acquired by Peace during his nocturnal prowls around London and elsewhere.

The new property had ample room to accommodate both parts of Peace's unconventional family. Hannah and Willie had 'two rooms upstairs and a back kitchen', while Peace and Sue had the rest of the house to themselves. This increased space no doubt reflected a desire for more domestic calm. The residence was also highly convenient for Peace's 'work' as the large back garden ran straight down to the Chatham and Dover railway line.

Even the most distinguished residents of the area were happy to be seen at Mr Thompson's popular musical evenings. Peace and Sue proved to be extremely hospitable hosts providing, as *The Times* later described it, 'a sumptuous table'. On these evenings of entertainment, Sue accompanied Peace on the piano as he played the violin or sang one of the sentimental ballads of the period. He also frequently enthralled their house guests by outlining his ideas for advances in the field of science and invention, which he now had the leisure and money to pursue.

He told his guests about the experiments he was conducting in his laboratory and of the new inventions he was working on: a smoke helmet for firemen, an improved brush for washing railway carriages and a form of hydraulic tank. Amazingly and surprisingly, this was all true. Inventing was an area of interest that Peace was pursuing with a new acquaintance called Mr Henry Forsey Brion.

Together Mr Thompson and Mr Brion had patented an invention for the raising of sunken vessels at sea by means of the displacement of the water inside the vessel using air and gas. It was noted in the *Patent Gazette* as '2635. Henry Forsey Brion, 22, Philip Road, Peckham Rye, London, S.E., and John Thompson, 5, East Terrace, Evelina Road, Peckham Rye, London, S.E., for an invention for raising sunken vessels by the displacement of water within the vessels by air or gases'.[86]

Peace made an 8ft long model ship which, using their compressed air system, they had managed to sink and then raise again three times in eight minutes. They also conducted large scale experiments in the Thames both near Westminster Bridge and London Bridge. It all looked very promising.

Encouraged by their success, the two inventors called on Mr Samuel Plimsoll, the Member of Parliament famous for his shipping interests, in order to garner his interest and support for their invention and, through him, to gain access to the First Lord of the Admiralty. They arrived at Mr Plimsoll's house in Park Lane announcing that they had 'a grand scheme for raising the *Vanguard*, the *Captain*, and the *Eurydice*'.[87]

Mr Plimsoll agreed to meet them the following day at the House of Commons. One of them met with him there in the outer lobby entrance of Westminster Hall, but the meeting did not prove to be very productive. They did not get to meet the First Lord of the Admiralty, as they had wished, and Mr Plimsoll requested that they write to his associate if they had anything further to tell him about their invention.[88] After that, they did write a number of letters to Mr Plimsoll's man, signed 'Brion and Co.'. In one of these letters they requested the names of any owners who had lost vessels on the western coast and, in response, were supplied with the name of a Greek ship that had been lost on Hooks Sands but for which £50 would have to be paid.

In the last letter that Mr Plimsoll's associate received from them, they asked if he would be willing to pay the £50 required, with a promise that they would refund him the amount at a later date. The letter does not seem to have elicited any response from the MP and that was the last time that they had any correspondence with Mr Plimsoll or his associates.[89] Mr Brion was impressed by Peace's talents in the area of science and invention and later wrote of him that he possessed 'great abilities' and had the ability to 'have made wealth and an honourable position in the world'.[90]

Apart from entertaining the neighbours and pursuing his love for music and science, Peace also found time to indulge his other interests. He liked to attend court cases and is said to have been present at one trial held at the Old Bailey during October and November of 1877, which dealt with a case known as 'the turf fraud scandal' where a number of policemen were found guilty of corruption.

As a respected member of the local community he liked to attend Sunday evening services at the parish church and expressed horror and outrage, along with everyone else, when an attempt was made to burgle the church.

Every night he continued his criminal work in the suburbs of London such as Blackheath, Streatham and Denmark Hill. He also ventured occasionally as far as Southampton, Portsmouth and Southsea. Sometimes he travelled on foot, in no way impeded by his limp, and other times, if the distance merited it, he used his pony and trap. He carried the tools of his trade concealed in a violin case and had a 5ft long steel bar, known as a jemmy, to force open doors and windows. His brace, with a collection of various size bits, and his large gimlet were used to make holes in doors and window frames.

If the owner of a property was foolish enough to leave a key in his door lock, Peace would use his small vice, or thumb screw, to turn the key from the outside and gain entry without having to force the door or even make holes in the wood.[91] He also carried his folding ladder, which when extended could reach over 12ft with a hook to facilitate attachment to the property but when contracted could be easily concealed. 'His ladder was quite a unique arrangement. When doubled up it is to all outward appearances simply a bundle of blocks of wood such as any carpenter might carry home for firewood.'[92] Even his small lantern, designed and made by himself, could fold up for convenient storage; he designed it so that it would project a narrow ray of light exactly where he pointed it and his finger could, in an instant, block all the light emanating from it. He also carried a chisel, a knife, a life preserver and, of course, his revolver.[93]

There are a number of anecdotes, some perhaps apocryphal, concerning Peace's activities from around this time. One concerns his local chemist who, when Peace entered his shop one day smoking a rather large cigar, asked him where he had got it. When Peace replied that it was stolen, the chemist laughed thinking that he was joking and said, 'I wish you'd steal a few for me'. 'Next time I come into the shop,' promised Peace, 'you shall have some.' Sure enough, true to his word, on his next visit to the chemist shop Peace duly supplied the man with a box of high-quality stolen cigars.

Then there is the story of the man he is said to have met on a train one day who was fascinated with the subject of crime. At first Peace was reluctant to become involved in the conversation, but the man persisted. Before long Peace had convinced him that he was a detective and they began to discuss the skills of the safe breaker. Peace claimed that, although he was not a professional burglar, he

The professional toolkit of Charles Peace. (Topfoto)

could break into any safe without being heard. He had learned the skill, he said, from doing his police work.

The man bet him £5 that he could not break into his safe without being detected. The arrangement was that the man would leave a handkerchief in his safe for the 'detective' to 'steal' and would stay in his bedroom unless he heard a sound. The man gave his address. The story goes that Peace entered the man's house that night, opened the safe and then closed it again with a loud bang. The man came down to find Peace standing there holding the handkerchief and admitting that he had been 'caught' in the act. They went on to have a glass or two of whisky before Peace handed over his fiver. Later, when Peace had left, the man realised that £150 was missing from his safe and the bet had been settled using one of his own £5 notes.

Peace himself told the story of how he spotted an unattended jewel case in a compartment of a stationary train one day as the owner and her servant had both left the carriage momentarily. He quickly snatched the case and made for the station exit. It was then that this fortuitous, opportunist robbery began to go awry when Peace noticed that the only exit from the station was manned by a police detective who, he feared, might recognise him.

He pondered his options in the knowledge that the robbery could be discovered any second. Having dismissed the idea of trying to make his way past the policeman or of hiding in some part of the building, Peace, as always, opted for the least likely mode of escape. He climbed up onto the roof of one of the train carriages and lay flat with the jewel case safely cocooned in his pocket. As the train pulled out of the station and began to gather speed he hung on desperately. With aching arms and having been almost choked to death by the thick smoke as the train travelled at high speed through a tunnel, Peace managed to hold on until the train came to a stop at the next station. He was glad to be able to climb down.

He did not, however, put as much distance between himself and the train as most thieves would have. Instead, he went to the ticket office and bought a first class ticket before re-entering the train. According to himself, he then made straight for the carriage from which he had taken the jewel case and sat opposite the victim. Satisfying his perverse sense of humour and bravado to the limit, he then engaged the poor woman in conversation and she gladly shared her sense of loss by telling him the whole story of how her jewels had just been stolen. All the time, of course, her jewels were ensconced only a few feet away in Peace's pocket.

No doubt his years of experience with jewellery had made him somewhat of an expert. This was borne out by another story. He was enjoying a day at the races, although his particular brand of entertainment came not from betting on horses but from the much more guaranteed earnings to be gleaned from robbing the punters. He managed to get himself close to one particularly rich looking mark and, before the man knew what was happening, had lifted an attractive gold chain from his pocket. He then found a quiet corner to examine his loot. With his knowledge of such things, Peace was not long in realising that the chain was nothing more than an admirable fake. The hallmark was a forgery and it was, in fact, a cheap brass chain that had received a gilding of gold. Not to be defeated, Peace made straight for a bookmaker. He told the man:

> I've put all I had on losers and now I haven't got so much as a bob left to try my luck again. What'll you give me for this chain? It's a real good 'un as you can see, stamped on every link. I only want a few pounds just to see if my luck turns. And the chain's worth a tenner to anyone at the very least.[94]

Without a word of a complaint, the man handed over £3 for the chain and was happy to be getting such a bargain.

These are just some of the stories and legends that were told about the exploits of Charles Peace at the time and contributed to his reputation as Britain's most infamous cat burglar. All the stories might not be true, but what we do know is that, just as he had in the North of England, Peace resisted any desire to become part of the underworld criminal community that existed in London at the time. He was a psychologically complex, independent-minded individual who, throughout his criminal career, preferred to work alone. His instinct told him that the more people involved in a criminal enterprise, the greater the risk of detection. As *The Times* newspaper put it: 'He … steered clear of the reef on which the majority of criminals have been wrecked, the treachery of confederates.'[95]

He did use his own small and trusted network of female associates who fenced stolen goods for him through pawnbrokers. When he stole jewellery, he would quickly remove the gemstones from the gold and silver so as to prevent their identification. Usually this was done on the very same night that they were stolen.[96] The gems could be sold easily and he would then melt down the gold and silver in a crucible and sell that by weight.[97]

Peace's life of opulence in London was put in danger one day when he ran suddenly into Detective Parrock, an old adversary, near the Holborn Viaduct. The two men recognised each other immediately. Peace ran and Parrock set off in chase. Although the detective almost had him at one point, Peace managed to escape.

It was also reported that, on two occasions, he ran into a man called Bill Fisher whom he knew from Yorkshire. The first time was again on the Holborn Viaduct and Peace heard his old acquaintance say to himself, 'Why, that's Peace'. The second time Peace was walking down Farringdon Road when their eyes met and Peace made a hasty retreat.[98] When Fisher went home to Sheffield he informed the local constabulary that he had seen Charles Peace in London, and the London police were made aware that the alleged murderer was in their city.[99]

Part 3

Luck Finally Runs Out — An Encounter with Constable Robinson

Constable Edward Robinson, PC 202 of the London Metropolitan Police Force R Division, was patrolling his beat after 2.00 a.m. on the morning of Thursday, 10 October 1878. The constable and his colleagues were on unusually high alert having come under pressure from their superiors to curb the recent spate of robberies that had been occurring in the Blackheath, Lee and Lewisham areas.[1]

The police had very little to go on, apart from the very small boot prints that had been left behind in the gardens of the properties targeted and the knowledge that they were dealing with someone who was both agile and cunning. So it was with particular interest that Constable Robinson, while in the avenue leading from St John's Park to Blackheath that night, noticed a faint flickering light in the drawing room window of 2 St John's Park.

The property was known as Gifford House and was the residence of Mr James Alexander Burness. The constable noticed that the light was moving from room to room and decided that it was worth investigating further. He got his colleague, Constable William Girling, to help him up onto the garden wall at the rear of the property. Sergeant Charles Brown then arrived on the scene and went round to the front of the house. Notwithstanding the lateness of the hour, the sergeant rang the front doorbell.

Inside the property, Charles Peace was hard at work. He had already 'bagged' a silver flask, a cheque book and an attractive letter case. He heard the doorbell just as he was about to do the same to some valuable plate, a crumb scoop, a sugar basin, a decanter stand and a spoon. Deciding that it was time to make his escape, Peace extinguished his lantern, hurried to the dining room and climbed out through the window into the back garden. Constable Robinson watched as this small man emerged lithely and gingerly from the house. The constable jumped off the wall and into the garden, unfortunately stepping on and breaking some glass as he did so. Peace heard the noise of the breaking glass and immediately began to run towards the back wall with Robinson in pursuit. When Robinson was within 6 yards of him, Peace turned and pointed his revolver at the constable's head, shouting, 'Keep back, keep off, or, by God, I will shoot you.'

'You had better not!' was Robinson's defiant reply.[2] He did not stop, but continued to approach his suspect. From the distance of about 2 yards, Peace fired three shots in quick succession, two of which passed to the left of the constable's head and the other directly over him. Robinson rushed for him and Peace fired again. This time Robinson felt the shot whizz past the right side of his head. The fact that the shots had, so far, missed their target was due only to the darkness of the night and not to any compassion on the part of Charles Peace. As Peace was taking aim once again, Robinson hit him in the face with his left hand, knocking him backwards. 'You bugger, I will settle you this time,' Peace shouted, and fired a fifth shot, aiming directly at the constable.[3]

Constable Robinson was hit. He had used his right arm to protect his head and the shot hit him just above the elbow. Blood began to flow from the wound in his arm, but being young, strong and eager, he was not to be denied his arrest. In spite of the injury, he managed to knock Peace to the ground and grab hold of his revolver. He failed to get complete possession of the weapon, however, as it was attached to Peace's wrist by a leather strap. Nevertheless, Robinson did manage to strike him over the head with it a number of times. Robinson then turned Peace over onto his front and held him there with his knee and his left hand until his fellow constables arrived.

The other constables came to his aid just in time, because by now Robinson was feeling faint from the loss of blood. His colleagues took over the tricky task of securing this violent burglar. Sergeant Brown hit Peace on the hand to get the revolver out of his grasp. 'I only did it to frighten him,' Peace said as he was being held down, 'so as I could get away.' The constables struggled to hold him. They were forced to hit him again a number of times to prevent him from escaping.

When the constables searched Peace they found the items that he had stolen from the house of Mr Burness along with a number of implements that they knew to be useful to a house breaker, such as an object that they described as a small crowbar found inside the pocket of his trousers. They also discovered a pocket knife, engraved upon which were the words 'Mr. Moss Isaacs, Herne Hill, Dulwich, shipbuilder'. Their investigation soon revealed that this knife had been stolen from Mr Isaacs' house months earlier.

Although Constable Robinson had got his man and would survive his injuries, he was quite seriously injured and would spend five weeks attending a surgeon for treatment. The bullet had travelled right through his arm. They didn't know it yet, but Robinson and his colleagues had just made the most important arrest of their careers.

The following morning Charles Peace was brought to appear before a magistrate at Greenwich Police Court. The problem for the police was that he was refusing to give his name and they had no idea who he was. As he was disguised with darkened skin, at first they were confused even about his race. The *London Daily Chronicle* carried the story:

> At Greenwich Police court yesterday a man about fifty years of age ... who refused his name and address, was charged with burglariously entering Gifford House, St. John's Park, Blackheath, and stealing silver and plated and other articles, and also with discharging five chambers of shot of a six chambered revolver and wounding Police constable Robinson, 202 R, by shooting him through the right arm.[4]

When asked for his name and address the prisoner's only reply was, 'Find out'.[5] The unknown dark-complexioned man was remanded for a week to be held in custody at Newgate Prison pending further inquiries.

True Identity Revealed

At first the police investigations failed to turn up anything at all on the mystery man who Constable Robinson had almost sacrificed his life to arrest. They even showed him to a number of prison warders and constables to find out if any of them knew who he was, but to no avail.[6] Then they got their first lead, when Peace asked for permission to write a letter. He was granted that permission and he wrote to his friend and co-inventor, Mr Brion. The mystery prisoner signed that letter, 'John Ward' and that is the name the police began to use for him.[7]

In his letter Peace told his friend that he had got himself into a predicament because of drink and that he did not know where his family was. He asked Mr Brion to pay him a visit. It is surprising that Peace chose to hand the police a lead in their investigation in this way but, perhaps, his obsessive and possessive nature had made him anxious about the whereabouts of his family. The fact of not knowing where Sue was, in particular, may well have been proving too much for him to bear.

The truth was, in fact, that when he failed to come home from his usual nocturnal travels, the women quickly put into action a plan that he had most likely devised for them himself. Fearing the worst, Sue and Hannah fled London and went first to the home of Sue's sister, Eliza Belfit, at North Street in Nottingham. They took a lot of luggage with them and had virtually stripped the house in Peckham of as many valuable items as they could carry. Eliza would later deny that she allowed them to stay with her, but did admit to holding on to a number of boxes for them.[8] A few days later Hannah moved on and went to Hazel Road in Sheffield where their daughter, Jane Ann, lived as Mrs Bolsover.

In response to the letter from Mr Ward, Mr Brion paid him a visit in Newgate Prison and was greatly surprised to find his friend John Thompson waiting for him.

The police, of course, lost no time in questioning Mr Brion about their mysterious prisoner. Mr Brion was shocked by what they told him and he co-operated by giving them all the information that he had. The constables now had the identity of Mr Thompson, the musical instrument dealer and inventor, as well as an address at Evelina Road.

As it happened, it was Peace himself who led them to the discovery of his true identity. On 5 November, he wrote a letter to Susan Gray, addressed to his 'dearly beloved wife' and addressing her as 'my dear Sue'. The constables paid her a visit. Peace, no doubt, expected her to stick with the 'Mr and Mrs Thompson' story, but she did not do so. Whether she gave in to police pressure, decided to betray her lover for the reward money or, for the first time, had no need to be afraid of Peace, she decided to tell them everything. She amazed the constables by telling them that the real name of their prisoner was Charles Peace.

Based on the information that they got from Sue, the constables then paid a visit to Peace's wife, Hannah, at Hazel Road in Sheffield. They knocked on the door and found a group of potential witnesses. They proceeded to interview Hannah, her son Willie, the daughter Jane Ann and the son-in-law, William Bolsover. They also interviewed Bolsover's sister, who was present. Then, in an unexpected bonus, Inspector Henry Phillips from the Criminal Investigation Department saw a clock in the room that he knew to be stolen from a Miss Dodson of Blackheath in London. When asked about this, Hannah Peace said, 'I did not know that it was stolen, a tall man gave it me about five weeks ago'.[9]

The truth about their prisoner was now being revealed to the police piece by piece. Hannah admitted that her name was Hannah Peace. The police searched the premises in Sheffield both on their initial visit and again some days later. They turned up many items that were stolen. A number of pawn tickets were found in the name of Thompson, most dated after Peace's arrest, and the constables knew that these were evidence of a desperate attempt on behalf of the women to get rid of some of the stolen goods.

A Constable Morris, who was acquainted with Peace, was brought from Sheffield to Newgate Prison in order to provide a definitive visual identification of their infamous prisoner. The constable was taken to the yard where the prisoners awaiting trial were exercising. As they passed him by, one by one, Constable Morris pointed to the fifth man, saying, 'That's Peace, I'd know him anywhere'.

When Peace saw the man pointing at him, he approached the prison officials and asked, 'What do you want me for?' He was ordered to continue with his exercise. He didn't know it yet, but his fate was sealed.

The newspapers, too, were keeping a close eye on what was happening. It was big news that the previously unidentified burglar who had almost killed Constable Robinson was actually Charles Peace, the man wanted for the Banner Cross murder. *The Times* carried the story of Peace's arrest: 'Information was yesterday received by the Chief Constable of Sheffield that Charles Peace, a picture frame dealer, who is alleged to have murdered Mr. Arthur Dyson, of Banner Cross, Sheffield, two years ago, had been arrested in London.'[10] The *Daily Telegraph* also informed its readers of the incredible news:

It is now established beyond all doubt that the burglar, captured by Police constable Robinson is one and the same as the Banner Cross murderer ... Numerous articles found in the houses of Peace's relatives have been identified by the owners from whose premises they were stolen during the last two years. A large number still remain unclaimed.[11]

The newspapers were hungry for any information that they could get about Peace and the arrest. The correspondent in the *Daily Telegraph* wrote, in particular, of 'a memorandum tablet in ivory and silver with a silver pencil-case' that had been found during police searches and had an inscription that showed another side to Peace's personality. The piece was given by Peace to his daughter on her birthday and the inscription read, 'Miss J. A. Peace. Given to her by her beloved father on her seventeenth birthday'.[12] It included a verse:

There is a flower, a gentle flower, that blooms in each shaded spot,
And gently to the heart it speaks – forget me not.
Love.

The *Daily Telegraph* told its readers that the police had found evidence to prove that a jewel robbery in Sheffield four years previously, in which £800 worth of goods had been stolen, was the work of Charles Peace. The police in London were relieved that the arrest of Peace would mean an end to the recent spate of robberies for which they had been coming under such pressure:

These burglaries, which have excited so much interest and even alarm in London, commenced in the early part of last winter, and were kept up with great regularity all through the season. The police received reports almost every Thursday and Saturday morning of burglaries at Blackheath, Lee, or Lewisham, and their utmost exertions failed to discover the perpetrator ... it was not until the 10th of October that he was seen by the police. He was then captured.[13]

The newspapers also reported that amongst the interesting material found by the police at Peace's residence was a plan of Camden Place, Chislehurst, the home in exile of the French Empress Eugénie and the Prince Imperial. This, the story claimed, brought to light an audacious scheme that was being plotted by Peace. According to the newspaper, Peace had written to the house explaining that it was his intention to build a large villa and, since 'Camden Place was admirably designed', he would like to visit there with his architect.[14] He would not, he explained, 'have taken this liberty, but he knew that the Empress and the Prince were abroad ...'[15] As the story went, the request was acceded to and Peace paid a visit to Camden Place in the company of another man, wherein he made a detailed diagram of the building and would, the press believed, have made ample use of it at some time in the future. *The Times* later claimed that there was no foundation to the story, so perhaps it is no more than another example of the mythical nature of Peace's reputation.[16]

The information and discoveries just kept coming. An amount of stolen stash, believed to be Peace's, was found by platelayers working on the London, Chatham, and Dover Railway line near Peace's house. The men unearthed a large trunk buried in the ground. When opened, it was found to contain a valuable assortment of treasures such as monogrammed plate that had been the property of an earl along with vases, paintings and around fifty gold and silver watches.

18

The Trial of Mr John Ward

Peace's trial for the assault on Constable Robinson took place under the name 'John Ward, alias Charles Peace', at the Old Bailey on 19 November 1878, before Mr Justice Hawkins.[17] The primary charge was of feloniously shooting at Constable Edward Robinson with intent to murder. He also faced charges of having intent to do grievous bodily harm, resisting lawful apprehension and burglary.

With the authorities still unsure about many of his personal details at the time of preferring charges, the 46-year-old Peace was listed in the calendar as being 60 years of age. Mr Montagu Williams, who led the prisoner's defence assisted by Mr William Austin Metcalfe, attempted to mitigate the charge by arguing that his client had only fired his pistol in order to frighten the constable and thus to facilitate his escape.

All three constables involved in the arrest were called to give their accounts of what had happened at Blackheath on the night in question. Constable Robinson was able to show the jury the coat that he had been wearing with the two holes that had been made in it by the passage of the shot that had wounded him. An Inspector Body was called and he stated that he had examined Mr Burness' property after the prisoner had been taken into custody:

> I found marks of the jemmy at the back dining-room window; it appeared as if it had been forced, the catch had been sprung and the window forced up. There was a hole in the dining-room door, about 5 inches square, large enough for a man's hand to be put through and undo it on the other side. In the library a desk had been forced and some drawers.[18]

A servant in the house, Sarah Selina Cooper, gave evidence to the effect that the day after the robbery she had found a bullet on the hearth rug while cleaning the dining room. She also said that there was a bullet hole in the centre of one of the windows.

Mr Montague Williams, in his closing statement on behalf of the defence, asked that the jury not be influenced by the fact that there had been many burglaries in the Blackheath area of late. They should not, he told them, allow that 'to operate against the prisoner'. They must, instead, consider the evidence. The prisoner, he told them, had no intention of murdering Constable Robinson. 'All he desired,' Williams said, 'was to escape, and … the facts themselves tended to support that view of the case.' If the prisoner was 'the desperate man he was reputed to be' and had he wanted the kill the constable, he could easily have done so. 'The pistol was not aimed at the chest or stomach of the officer,' Williams reminded them, 'but over his head and at his side, and … the shots were fired merely to frighten him.'

Justice Hawkins' concise and logical summing up of the case did not assist Mr Montague Williams and his client with their claims of innocence. The justice considered the matter to be fairly straightforward. As to the prisoner being engaged in burglary, 'There was no doubt whatever that on the morning in question a burglary was committed at Mr. Burness's house and that the prisoner jumped from the window'.[19] This meant that the constable was 'thoroughly justified in apprehending the prisoner on the charge of having committed that burglary'.[20] It was also quite clear that the prisoner had discharged his weapon at the constable:

> … the prisoner had fired five shots from a revolver at the constable … and the only question was as to the intent with which the shots were fired. If the prisoner meant only to frighten the officer, he could have done so with a pistol charged with powder only, and he had no need, if that was his object, to have used powder and ball.[21]

Once they had heard all the evidence and statements, the jury members left the courtroom for only four minutes before returning with a verdict of guilty. Peace appeared to be greatly affected by the decision; it was said by Montagu Williams that he 'completely broke down, and his bearing upon the occasion … was far from suggestive of the man of courage he most certainly was'.[22] One would have to wonder whether this show of emotion was merely a ploy on his behalf to gain mercy from the court.

He was invited by Justice Hawkins to say if there was any reason why he should not be sentenced. Peace took the opportunity of addressing the court and made a statement in what was said to be 'a whining tone, with tears in his eyes, and almost grovelling on the floor'.[23] He complained that the court had not been fair to him:

I have not been fairly dealt with, and I declare before God that I had never any intention to kill. All I meant to do was to frighten him, so as I might get away. If I'd wanted to kill him I could easily have done it, but I never did.[24]

He denied that he fired five shots at Constable Robinson. As if it represented a significant lessening in the severity of his crime, he claimed indignantly to have 'only fired four'. What is more, he said that he could prove it was an accident:

If your lordship will look at the pistol, your lordship will see that it goes off very easily, and the sixth barrel went off of its own accord after I was taken into custody. At the time the fifth shot was fired the constable had hold of me, and the pistol went off quite by accident. I really did not know that the pistol was loaded.[25]

Nevertheless, Peace did admit that he had done wrong and pleaded for mercy:

I hope, my lord, you will have mercy upon me. I know that I am base and bad. I feel that I am that base and bad that I am neither fit to live nor die. For I have disgraced myself. I have disgraced my friends, and I am not fit to live among mankind. I am not fit to meet my God, for I am not prepared to do so. So, oh, my Lord, I know I am base and bad to the uttermost, but I know, at the same time, they have painted my case blacker than it really is. I hope you will take all this into consideration, and not pass upon me a sentence of imprisonment which will be the means of causing me to die in prison, where it is very possible I shall not have a chance amongst my associates to prepare myself to meet my God that I hope I shall meet. So, my lord, do have mercy upon me. I beseech you, give me a chance, my lord, to regain my freedom, and you shall not, with the help of my God, have any cause to repent passing a merciful sentence upon me. Oh, my lord, you yourself do expect mercy from the hands of your great and merciful God. Oh, my lord, do have mercy upon me, a most wretched, miserable man – a man that am not fit to die.

He promised the justice that, if treated leniently, he would be good in the future:

I am not fit to live; but with the help of my God I will try to become a good man. I will try to become a man that will be able in the last day to meet my God, my Great Judge, to meet Him and to receive the great reward at His hands for my true repentance. So, oh, my lord, have mercy upon me, I pray and beseech you. I will say no more; but, oh, my lord, have mercy upon me; my lord, have mercy upon me.[26]

It seems that Mr Justice Hawkins remained unmoved by the quality of Peace's oratory. According to Montagu Williams, the justice may have been alone in this lack of emotion, '[It] seemed to have an effect upon everybody in court except the man to whom it was addressed. It was a great treat to watch the face of Mr. Justice Hawkins during the speech.'[27]

When Peace was finished, Mr Justice Hawkins said that he was in agreement with the verdict reached by the jury:

> You were detected in the act of committing a burglary, and, putting altogether aside what may have been your conduct on other occasions, the circumstances of this particular case are quite sufficient to prove to my mind that you are an accomplished burglar, and that you went to this house, determined to rob, by fair means if you could, but armed in a manner that show you were also determined to resort to foul means if necessary to escape detection.[28]

The justice rejected Peace's argument of having fired the shots only to frighten Constable Robinson and effect an escape:

> You have asserted that you only fired the pistol at the constable in order to frighten him, that thus you might be enabled to make your escape. I do not believe you. A man who has a deadly instrument of this description strapped to his arm does not make use of it in the manner you did without a deadly intention; it is beyond belief that he can have any other.

The justice told him that he was lucky not to be facing a murder charge:

> ... the prosecutor, and you, also, have to thank God the constable's life was spared. In the discharge of his duty, and, in the bravest manner, he advanced to close with you, and while he was near to you, four shots were deliberately fired at him, and, if one thing was wanting to show your murderous intention it was supplied by the expression made use of by you before you fired the fifth shot, 'I will settle you this time'. This shot was fired at his head, and, but that he was guarding his head at the time with his arm, he would have received the shot upon it, and, if that had been the case, death would most likely have been the result, and you at this moment would probably be receiving sentence of death.[29]

Mr Justice Hawkins sentenced Peace to penal servitude for the rest of his natural life. By now, any sympathy that the crowd in court had been developing for the plight of 'Mr Ward' had obviously dissipated and the sentence was greeted by spontaneous applause. Mr Justice Hawkins called for silence.

The jury members had composed a note in which they complimented Constable Robinson on his courageous actions and recommended that 'his conduct … be recognised and rewarded'.[30] Justice Hawkins concurred with this view and called the constable forward. 'He strongly recommended him for promotion, and said he was a man of whom the whole force might be proud.'[31]

Hawkins duly granted the constable a reward of £25. The people who lived in Blackheath and the surrounding neighbourhoods were also appreciative of the diligence and bravery that had been demonstrated by Robinson and his colleagues in arresting Peace. They awarded Robinson 'a handsome watch and chain' along with 25 guineas; Sergeant Brown and Constable Girling received £5 each for their efforts on the night.[32]

The Trial of Hannah Peace

Charles Peace was not the only one in trouble with the law. As such a large quantity of items stolen by Peace had been discovered in his wife Hannah's possession, she too found herself facing prosecution. She was charged, on 7 November 1878, with having received stolen property and she was remanded on a number of occasions. She was brought to Bow Street in London on 18 December to a hearing before the magistrate, Mr Vaughan. The prosecution was led by Mr Poland, assisted by Mr Tickell; Hannah was represented by Mr Beard Jnr. Her defence was based on an existing legal precedent which stated that 'if a wife, in removing property alleged to be stolen, had acted with the motive of saving her husband from peril, a charge of felony could not be sustained'.[33]

The problem was, however, that although Hannah claimed to be Peace's wife she was unable to produce any legal evidence to prove the fact. The prosecution pointed out that both the registers at Somerset House and the parish in Sheffield had been searched and no record of the marriage could be found. On the contrary, in fact, it was well known in the area of London where they lived, that Peace always referred to another woman, Mrs Susan Thompson, as his wife; the accused, they said, was known as Mrs Ward. The prosecution claimed that the alleged marriage between the accused and Mr Peace had not taken place and, consequently, her 'dealings with the stolen property were those of an accomplice'.[34]

The first person called to give evidence at the hearing was Emma Shapley, the wife of William Shapley of Seymour Lodge, Peckham Rye. In answer to Mr Tickell's question she explained that she had noticed a number of items of clothing missing from their house on 23 September. It seems that a servant had left a door open earlier in the evening and someone had entered and taken 'seven pocket handkerchiefs, a night dress, a pair of slippers, two scarves, and a pair of silk stockings'.[35] These items had all been found in Hannah's possession.

Other witnesses followed with similar stories. They had all lost property, which had been stolen by Peace and was found in Hannah's possession. Mrs Sarah Boucher's housekeeper, Eliza Macdonald, said that when she began work on the morning of 11 August she found that the breakfast room window in her mistress's house had been forced open and a number of items had been stolen, including a silver pickle fork and an Indian manufactured tablecloth, both of which were produced as evidence in court.[36]

Jacob Eavis, gardener to Mr Frederick Stanley of Arbutus Lodge, Denmark Hill, testified that one day the previous September, while his employer was away, he noticed that the house had been broken into. When Mr Stanley returned home from Brighton he found that property to the value of £50 was missing, comprising of dessert knives, a fork and a pair of bracelets, all of which were shown in court and all said to have been found in Hannah's possession. 'A quantity of silver and electro plate' was also produced in court and identified as the property of Mr W. B. Tidd, of Upper Denmark Hill, by his parlour maid, Louisa Tween.[37] She testified that it had all been stolen on 18 September. The thief, she said, had forced the window to her master's bedroom from the outside.[38]

Police Inspectors Phillips and Bonney gave evidence of finding all the stolen items in Hannah's possession.[39] Inspector John Pinder Twybell gave evidence regarding the clock, stolen from a house in Blackheath, that he had seen in the house of the prisoner's daughter, Mrs Bolsover. He told the court that when he put this to the prisoner she claimed to know nothing about its theft. William Bolsover, the son-in-law, was also called to give evidence and he gave an interesting insight into Charles Peace's unusual living arrangements:

On Whit Monday last I came to London and went to 5 Evelina Road ... where I found Peace living with a woman, and they passed as Mr. and Mrs. Thompson. The prisoner [Hannah] was there living as Mrs. Ward, and the young man as Willie Ward. I stayed in the house with my wife eight or nine days ... While there I took my meals with the prisoner and Willie Ward. Mr. and Mrs. Thompson had theirs separately.[40]

Bolsover was asked to identify the woman known as Mrs Susan Thompson, who was in court in the company of a constable, which he did. He told the court that after Peace had been arrested, Hannah and Willie came to stay at his house in Sheffield. Hannah had told him 'that she had read in the papers of a man being apprehended, and she thought it was her husband'.[41] He stated that they brought a large amount of goods with them to his house.

Eliza Belfit, who was Susan Gray's sister, told the court how her sister and the prisoner had arrived at her house one night in October.[42] Her sister introduced the prisoner to her as 'Mrs Ward'. The prisoner told her that they had been living together and were in trouble. She said that she agreed to store some boxes for them in her house and went with them to the train station. She denied under cross-examination that she was aware that her sister 'lived with a man named Peace and assisted him in committing burglaries'.[43]

The determination of the magistrate was that there were grounds for Hannah Peace to be sent forward to full trial. Peace had tried to exonerate her by writing a letter to the Chief Commissioner of Police in which he said she was innocent and saying of the loot found in her possession, 'she knows nothing of me having stolen it'.[44] Nevertheless, Hannah's trial went ahead on 14 January 1879, at the Old Bailey. The official charge was of 'feloniously receiving seven pocket handkerchiefs and a quantity of other articles, the proceeds of different burglaries committed in the neighbourhood of Blackheath last year by a man named Peace, who she alleged was her husband, well knowing the same to be stolen'.[45]

Hannah's defence at the trial, this time led by Mr Fulton, was still based upon the argument that she was married to Charles Peace and had only acted at all times under his coercion in these matters. Her greatest difficulty was caused by the fact that she was still unable to produce a legal marriage certificate. She told the court that 'her old man' had burned it and the witnesses to the marriage, named as John and Clara Clark, were dead.[46]

Once again a number of witnesses were brought forward to testify regarding their property that had been stolen and then found in the prisoner's possession. Some had already given evidence at the previous hearing. The evidence gave an idea of the range and scope of Peace's burglary during that time in London. Mrs Emma Shapley testified that wearing apparel to the value of £23 had been stolen from their house on 23 September. Frederick Stanley of Denmark Hill told of how he had been deprived of 'two dessert knives, one dessert fork, and a pair of bracelets'.[47] Louisa Newman, cook to a Mr Charles Thomas Perry of Forest Hill, said that on 5 August two caskets, a tortoiseshell, a cornelian and other items, all to the value of £30 or £40, were stolen from her master's house. The daughter of Mr Campbell Dadson identified a clock that had been stolen from her father's property along with 'much more valuable property'.[48] All of these stolen items had been found on Hannah and were produced as evidence in court.

Peace's fellow inventor and friend Mr Brion gave evidence that, although a frequent visitor to her house in Peckham, he had never heard the prisoner referred to as Peace's wife. To him she was always Mrs Ward and 'Mrs Thompson was introduced as Mr. Thompson's wife'.[49]

Hannah's legal team didn't contest any of the evidence regarding the property in question, that it was stolen, or that it was found in her possession; they continued to argue that she did not know anything about the origins of these items and that, most important of all, she had acted at all times on her husband's instructions. In the end the court agreed with the submission of Hannah's counsel and ruled that the prosecution had failed to disprove the existence of a legal marriage between her and Charles Peace. It was, therefore, the legal view that she had acted under her husband's coercion and had no case to answer. The jury was directed to find Hannah not guilty and she was discharged.

20

A Murder Charge

Now that the authorities had been successful in their prosecution of Charles Peace for his attack on Constable Robinson, they were determined to bring him to justice for the murder of Arthur Dyson at Banner Cross as well.

The press, too, were eagerly anticipating a follow-up trial and were prejudging the outcome as is evident from a piece published in *The Times* just the day after his conviction for the shooting of Constable Robinson: 'The case created considerable interest, the prisoner, it is said, being the murderer of a Mr Dyson at Banner Cross, near Sheffield, some years ago, under circumstances which then caused intense excitement and which since have been enveloped in mystery.'[50]

Following her husband's murder, Katherine Dyson had gone on a trip back to her friends and relatives in Cleveland, Ohio, in an attempt to cope with all that had happened to her. However, as the only witness to the shooting in Banner Cross that night, the police needed her back in England to testify against Peace.

At the time of her husband's murder it was thought prudent to give her police protection, as it was feared that Peace might try to kill her. Police Constable Walsh from Sheffield was assigned the job at the time, perhaps because of his Irish heritage and because he had spent ten years living in Cleveland.[51] The authorities knew that she had got on well with Walsh and trusted him, so he was dispatched to America in order to bring her back to England. Katherine agreed to return and testify, so Katherine and Constable Walsh travelled back on the White Star steamer *Britannic* into Liverpool and arrived in Sheffield in early January 1879.[52] Police Inspector Bradbury met them at the station and brought Katherine to stay at his own home for the duration of the proceedings against Peace.

On 13 January 1879 she was taken to London where she had a meeting with the solicitor for the Treasury, followed by a visit to Newgate Prison for the purpose of positively identifying her old friend, Charles Peace.

When Peace became aware that he was to be charged with the murder of Arthur Dyson, he wrote a letter to the Secretary of State from Newgate Prison pleading for leniency and requesting access to all the evidence against him.[53] The letter, dated 25 November 1878, is interesting because it contains numerous spelling mistakes and errors of grammar, which makes it like most of the original documents believed to have been handwritten by Peace, and unlike the notes found in the field across from the Dysons' house. If this letter is indicative of Peace's actual writing abilities, he could not have forged the notes that purport to have come from Katherine Dyson. Could the poor writing be a ploy on his part intended to elicit sympathy for the plight of a poor, illiterate, ignorant man? It is also possible, of course, that he could have got someone else to forge the Katherine Dyson notes for him, such as his daughter for example. If this letter to the Home Secretary is an example of his true writing ability, it explains why he had got Arthur Dyson to write out his picture framing receipts for him.

Peace used this letter to the Secretary of State to make a number of accusations against the prosecution's main witness. One of the claims he made was that Katherine Dyson was not really Arthur Dyson's wife at all, but just some woman that Dyson had brought over with him from America. He said that he [i.e. Peace] had been 'cohabiting' with her himself and that there were photographs in existence and the handwritten notes to prove that. He pointed out that the relationship between Arthur Dyson and Katherine had been a turbulent and violent one and that Arthur Dyson had even pointed a pair of pistols at his wife through their bedroom window and threatened to kill both her and Peace. He also claimed that Katherine, in front of witnesses, had threatened to kill her husband 'before she had don [sic] with him'.[54] It was already known to the police that there was truth to Peace's accusation of a fiery relationship having existed between the Dysons and that Katherine was not very happily married.

At 9.00 a.m. on Friday, 17 January 1879, the process of bringing Peace to justice for the death of Mr Arthur Dyson began. He was taken from Pentonville Prison, London, where he was then serving his sentence, and brought to a hearing at the town hall in Sheffield, presided over by the stipendiary magistrate, Mr E.M.E. Welby. The purpose of such a hearing was to determine whether there was sufficient cause for the prisoner to stand trial for murder.

Although Peace had only been told about the hearing the day before and his legal advisor appointed that very morning, the local people of Sheffield had obviously found out about it; so large was the crowd trying to gain entry to the town hall that the police had to block the doors in order to prevent people from forcing their way in.[55] This interest in Peace's case was replicated nationally: 'The case has excited great interest throughout the country, not only in consequence of the escape of the murderer, but owing to his daring burglaries in different parts of the kingdom.'[56]

Peace, dressed in his convict uniform, was placed in the dock at noon and formally charged with the murder of Mr Arthur Dyson at Banner Cross. His legal representative was Mr William Clegg who, at that time, was a celebrity in his own right as an international football player for England. Both Clegg and his brother, Charles, were capped for England. He later became Lord Mayor of Sheffield. Mr Pollard conducted the prosecution on behalf of the Treasury.

Clegg's determined reputation on the football field would soon be replicated in the courtroom during his robust cross-examination of Katherine Dyson. One of Mr Clegg's first acts was to call for an adjournment of the hearing on the grounds that neither he nor his client had received sufficient notice:

> … I was only instructed this morning to appear in this case. It has been a matter of utter impossibility for me to have got full instructions from the man, seeing that I was only instructed about ten o'clock this morning in the matter. I understand that the prisoner has only been brought down from London this morning, and therefore it has been impossible for me to have communication with him earlier or that I could have had a personal interview with him before.[57]

William Clegg, lawyer and international football player, was so busy defending Charles Peace that he was late for the start of a match in which he had been picked to play for England. (Topofoto)

Clegg's application was denied by the magistrate and the proceedings got under way. Mr Pollard, in his opening statement on behalf of the prosecution, pointed out that following the murder of Mr Dyson Charles Peace had continued with his life of crime for two years until he was eventually captured in the act of burglary. Mr Clegg objected immediately. He said it was out of order to mention any other crimes that his client was alleged to have committed. A legal discussion ensued between the stipendiary magistrate, Mr Clegg and Mr Pollard on the matter:

Clegg: 'I object to this; it has nothing to do with the present charge.'[58]

Magistrate [to Mr Pollard]: 'You had better not go into that now.'

Pollard: 'But the man was then taken into custody.'

Clegg: 'I object to that; we are not charged with any offence committed then.'

Magistrate [to Pollard]: 'Why take the other case? Why not go on at once with this charge?'

Pollard: 'I simply wished to say that whilst engaged in the commission of another offence he was taken into custody.'

Clegg: 'I object to any remarks on that subject.'

Pollard: 'He is here as a convict in a convict dress.'

Magistrate: 'We must go back to November 1876.'

Mr Pollard agreed to relent and proceeded to call Katherine Dyson as his witness. Katherine made her way to the witness box dressed in the traditional black garb of the Victorian widow. No sooner had she been sworn in than Peace objected loudly from the dock, demanding that she be sworn in again. His objection was based on the fact that she was wearing a veil and had not, therefore, kissed the Bible in the correct manner. 'Will you be kind enough to take your veil off?' Peace said to her directly: 'You have not kissed the book.' The court asked Katherine to comply with his request. She removed the veil calmly from her face and kissed the Bible again.

In reply to Mr Pollard's questions, Katherine began to give details of her dealings with Charles Peace. She explained how Peace had been a neighbour of herself and her husband when they lived in Darnall. She and her husband had got to know him first, she explained, in his professional capacity as a picture framer, when he framed four pictures for them. She said that he continued to call on them after that, even though her husband did not like him at all and eventually asked him to stop doing so. She told the court how relations became so bad between them that Peace had threatened her with a pistol and that she and her husband had been left with no option but to have a legal summons issued against him. When he didn't show up to answer the summons in court, a warrant was issued for his arrest. Katherine told how, even after they moved to Banner Cross in order to get away from him, Peace continued to harass them at their new address.

Pollard led Katherine through her version of the events as they happened on the night of her husband's death; she told how Peace had accosted her in their back yard with a gun, how she had screamed causing Arthur to come out and how

Peace had shot her husband before running away. At one point Peace said that he could not hear her evidence and she was told to speak up by Mr Pollard so that the prisoner could hear what she was saying.

When the prosecution had concluded with their questioning of Katherine Dyson, Mr Clegg asked that he be permitted to defer his cross-examination of her until a later time. This request was granted and they moved on to the next witnesses for the prosecution. Mrs Mary Ann Gregory, the shopkeeper, told how she had seen Mr Peace twice. The first time was on the night that the Dysons moved to Banner Cross at the end of October; she told how he had come into their shop, engaged her husband in conversation and bought some tobacco. The next time, she told the court, was on the night of Mr Dyson's death when he came in looking for her husband. She saw him later walking near the Dysons' house. Mrs Gregory testified how she later heard the sound of Mrs Dyson screaming and what sounded like gunshots. She found out that Arthur Dyson had been shot when she went to their house and, she said, 'saw him sitting in a chair with blood streaming from his head'.[59]

At one point during Mrs Gregory's testimony Peace interrupted proceedings to complain about someone in court who, he said, was sketching his portrait. He was informed that the man in question was just a reporter from a newspaper and would not take his portrait if he objected to it. It turned out, in any event, that the man was only taking notes and not sketching at all.[60]

After this latest interruption from Peace, the hearing continued with Sarah Colgreaves' testimony about speaking with the prisoner on the evening of Mr Dyson's death and how, in conversation with her, he had 'threatened to kill "the strangers"', by which he meant the Dysons. Peace's legal representative tried to cast doubt on Sarah Colgreaves' ability to remember what the man looked like and to recognise him again, having only seen him in the dark. As that was going on, Peace pulled what was described as 'a horrible facial contortion' and proceeded to ask the witness whether he looked like that on the night. The magistrate told him to remain quiet. This caused Peace to become very agitated and to address the magistrate directly:

> I beg your pardon, sir, but my life is at stake, and I am going to vindicate my character as well as I can. If you don't want me to speak, put a gag in my mouth. When I hear a person perjuring herself I will speak. I wish to say it openly and in court that up to the time when this woman saw me in Newgate I had disfigured my face so as not to be known. I was not then known as Charles Peace, and I had disfigured my face so that I had deceived all the detectives in London. My face was disfigured when this woman saw me.[61]

The next witness called was the local labourer Charles Brassington who explained that he also met the prisoner on the night of the murder. He said that when Peace asked him, 'Have you any strange people come to live about here?', he told him that he did not know.[62] He then told the court how Peace had shown him a number of photographs and some letters, saying, 'I will make it a warm one for these strangers before morning. I will shoot them both.'[63] Peace became infuriated on hearing Brassington's evidence. Once again he interrupted proceedings, shouting out, 'Oh, you false man! I never said so.'[64] He demanded justice from the court:

> I am not a dog. My life is at stake. If you hang me it will only free me from a long, dreary, life of penal servitude, and I don't care much which way it is; but I am going to have full justice done me. I will interrupt you if you do not do justice, and if you gag me I'll try to interrupt you.[65]

Mr Pollard, on behalf of the prosecution, objected to these repeated interruptions by the prisoner and reminded the stipendiary magistrate that he had the power to remove the prisoner from court if necessary. The magistrate replied that he wished to be fair to the prisoner and, if possible, he did not wish to use that power.

Eventually Peace quietened down and the proceedings were able to resume. The prosecution called Thomas Wilson, who said that he had seen a man run from the scene that night and had gone to the Dysons' house when he heard Katherine's screams. James William Harrison, the surgeon who had attended the fatally wounded Arthur Dyson, was called to give evidence and he produced the actual bullet that had killed Mr Dyson. Two policemen, Constable George Ward and Inspector Jacob Bradbury, also gave evidence, in the course of which the handwritten notes that had been found in the field across from the Dysons' house were produced in court.[66]

Once the case for the prosecution had come to its conclusion, it was decided that the hearing would be adjourned until the following week, at which point Mr Clegg would be given his opportunity of cross-examining Katherine Dyson and introducing witnesses if he so desired. As Peace left Sheffield for the trip back to London, large crowds had gathered at the station to catch a glimpse of him. There was no doubt that even bigger crowds would await the second sitting.

21

Bid for Freedom

Peace's hearing before the stipendiary magistrate was scheduled to reconvene at 10.00 a.m. on 22 January. That morning a large and excited crowd waited at the station and around Sheffield town hall, in the hope of seeing the arrival of Britain's most notorious villain. At this point Peace was being held on remand at Pentonville Prison in London. He was to be transported on the 5.15 a.m. Great Northern newspaper train from King's Cross Station, and due to arrive in Sheffield at 8.45 a.m. The prisoner was seen to board the train in London, bound by handcuffs and in the custody of warder William Roberson and chief warder at Pentonville Prison, James Cosgrove.

There was great shock amongst those in the courtroom at Sheffield when Mr Jackson, the chief constable, suddenly came in and announced to all those assembled that Charles Peace had escaped from custody on the journey from London.[67] He informed his shocked listeners that, for the present, no other details were available.

As shocking as the chief constable's announcement was, it did not do justice to the drama that had unfolded on the train from London that morning. On the previous journey to Sheffield the week before Peace had been obstreperous and, once again, this morning the prison warders found him a handful from the beginning. When they let him out of the train to get some air and 'stretch' his legs at Peterborough Station, he refused to re-enter the carriage and had to be forced to do so physically before a crowd of shocked onlookers. Very early into the train journey Peace announced that he was feeling unwell. Every time the train stopped, he made the excuse that he had to leave the carriage in order to be sick or relieve himself. The two custodians charged with the responsibility of getting him to

Sheffield decided after some time that they had had enough of this nuisance and got some little bags for Peace to use instead of having to leave the train. The used bags could then be thrown out of the train window.

The train had passed through Worksop and was somewhere between Shireoaks Station and Kiveton Park Station when Peace asked for one of these 'sick' bags. When the warder lowered the window in order to allow him to throw the used bag out, Peace took a flying leap through the open window. William Roberson just managed to grab hold of Peace's left foot before he was clear of the train.

Peace was now hanging from the carriage window by one foot, grasping the footboard and kicking the warder with his free foot. At this time the train was travelling somewhere between 40–50 miles per hour.[68] Soon the warder's hand was bleeding from the kicks he was receiving, but he was doing his best to hold on. At the same time the chief warder, James Cosgrove, was pulling the communication cord in a frantic attempt to get the train to stop, but with little effect. Peace was carried this way for 2 miles until, finally, he managed to free himself from his left shoe and fell down heavily beside the tracks.

The train continued on for another mile before it finally came to a halt. The frantic prison officials ran back along the line in search of their prisoner. Near Kiveton Park they found him lying in the snow, only semi-conscious and bleeding from a deep wound in his head. Although injured, Peace had managed to free one of his hands from the handcuffs. As soon as he came fully to his senses all he said was, 'I am cold; cover me up'.[69]

Back in Sheffield, the chief constable made an announcement through the window of the town hall to make the waiting public in the street below aware that Peace had escaped. He had no sooner done so, however, than a piece of paper was thrust into his hand from which he was able to inform his listeners that the prisoner had been recaptured and was on his way to Sheffield after all. This second announcement was greeted with a loud cheer. What they did not know yet was that Peace was in no condition to continue with his hearing that day.

Peace was put into the guard's van of the next train and brought the rest of the way to Sheffield. He had to be carried to a cell at the police station by four men. A doctor was called to tend to his injuries. At first he was barely able to take the brandy prescribed for him by the doctor and was very weak from the loss of blood. His attempted escape, it seems, had only added to his notoriety: 'Peace has become more notorious than ever. The streets in the neighbourhood of the police station and the town hall have been crowded with spectators, eager to learn the least bit of intelligence as to his condition, for several hours.'[70]

But then there was another twist in the story when news began to leak out that perhaps it had not been an attempted escape at all. A note, written in pencil, had been found on the injured prisoner – 'Bury me at Darnall. God Bless you all. – C. Peace'.

Was the jump an attempted suicide? At least one newspaper correspondent speculated that it had been a vain attempt by Peace to end his life: 'His object was to commit suicide, and, singular to say, the attempt was made only a few miles from the spot where Peace has often of late desired that he should be buried.'[71]

Perhaps the note was written just in case the worse happened. Peace knew better than most people that an attempted jump from a moving train was a dangerous feat and that he may well end up dead. Peace himself, in a letter written to his stepson some time later, would later claim that it was a suicide attempt:

> I saw from the way I was guarded all the way down from London, and all the way back, when I came for my first trial, that I could not get away from the warders, and I knew I could not jump from an express train without being killed. I took a look at Darnall as I went down and as I went back; and after I was put in my cell I thought it over. I felt that I could not get away, and then I made up my mind to kill myself. I got two bits of paper, and I pricked on one of them the words, 'Bury me at Darnall. God bless you all'. With a bit of black dirt that I found on the floor in my cell I wrote the same words on another piece of paper, and then I hid them in my clothes. My hope was that when I jumped from the train I should be cut to pieces under the wheels … As soon as the inquest was over you would have claimed the body, found the pieces of paper, and then you would have buried me at Darnall.[72]

He said the same in a letter to Sue on 26 January: 'I am very ill from the effects of the jump from the train. I tried to kill myself to save all further trouble and distress, and to be buried at Darnall.'[73]

In light of this latest incident on the train, Peace was determined to be too much of a security risk to be sent back to London, so it was decided to keep him in Sheffield until the preliminary hearing could be brought to a conclusion. He was placed under constant observation in his cell.[74] He soon began to recover from his injuries and when visited by his solicitor was fit enough to complain vehemently about the witness, Mr Brassington, who he claimed had perjured himself at the first session.

22

The Continuation of the Hearing

Peace was declared medically fit to appear at the continuation of his hearing before the stipendiary magistrate, Mr Welby, rescheduled for 24 January 1879. Because of the added security threat that Peace was now regarded as posing, and the ever increasing interest amongst the general public in the case, it was decided to hold the next session in a corridor of the Central Police Station, under candlelight and without an audience. This new venue had the added advantage of being only a short walk from the cell in which Peace was being held. The idea was that, apart from the legal officers, only the press and the witnesses would be informed of the venue in advance. The general public, in the mistaken belief that he was to appear at the town hall that morning, gathered in their thousands around that building.[75]

At 10.00 a.m. Peace, sporting a large bandage on his head, was carried from his cell and placed sitting in a chair at the end of a table. He was greatly surprised and, being the exhibitionist that he was, expressed his extreme dissatisfaction with the new venue. 'What is this?' he protested loudly.[76]

He was informed by the stipendiary magistrate that this was where the remainder of his hearing would be held. Peace told the magistrate that he would not be able to stand it and that he was very cold. 'I ought not to be brought here,' he complained. The magistrate insisted that he would have to make do with the new arrangement: 'You must do the best you can do. This is only the preliminary inquiry. You are not absolutely obliged to be here, so you must attend as well as you can. You are represented here, and the preliminary inquiry is to be finished today.'[77]

It was noticed by many of those present how ill Peace looked on this occasion.[78] 'I wish to God there was something across my shoulders,' he said. 'I am very cold. Oh, dear; oh, dear!'[79] He was provided with some rugs to keep him warm, but still continued to complain. 'I am not able to go on; I am not.' 'This is not justice.' 'Why does not my solicitor prevent this and let me have a remand?'[80]

Addressing Mr Clegg directly, he said, 'Why don't you ask for a remand?' The magistrate intervened to tell him that he could not have a remand and that he should not exhaust himself in this way. Peace continued to rant for a minute or two about not being granted a remand, before proceedings could finally get under way.

The hearing had reached a point that was eagerly anticipated by all – the imminent confrontation between Katherine Dyson and Peace's counsel and local football hero, Mr William Clegg. Before being cross-examined by Clegg, Katherine was instructed to answer a few extra questions from Mr Pollard for the prosecution. These questions dealt with two photographs.

In her replies she acknowledged that she did have her photograph taken with the prisoner at Sheffield Fair in 1876 and that photograph was produced in court. At that time, she said, she believed the prisoner to be 'a respectable man'.[81] Then there was another smaller photograph of Katherine herself, suitable for placing in a locket, which had been taken some time earlier in America. When asked about this small image, Katherine stated that she had kept it in a locket on her mantelpiece but that it had gone missing. It was discovered by the police along with Peace's belongings in his daughter's house.[82]

As Katherine was giving her evidence, Peace once again began to disrupt proceedings. At one point he put his legs up on the table in front of him and was told by the magistrate, 'You must not put your feet on the table, Sir'.

He replied, 'All right, Sir', and took them down. Later, he demanded that a milkman, who he claimed had delivered notes between himself and Katherine Dyson, be called to give evidence. On yet another occasion, when he asked that a policeman called David be called, his solicitor told him to be quiet. He continued to mutter to himself unhappily for some time.

Mr Clegg now rose for his cross-examination of Katherine Dyson. This interaction would become particularly intriguing due to Clegg's focus upon the potentially scandalous handwritten notes that had been found in the field across from the Dysons' house. Clegg had obviously come to the conclusion that the best way to achieve a lesser charge against his client was to prove that Katherine and Peace had been on much more intimate terms than she was admitting and, thus, to undermine her credibility as a witness.

This would also suggest to the jury that Arthur Dyson had good reason to be a jealous husband and was, in fact, the aggressor on that fatal night at Banner Cross and not Peace. Peace, he was trying to argue, had acted in self-defence and the death of Arthur Dyson had been the result of an accidental discharge of the gun during a physical struggle. As one newspaper put it, these written notes could cast 'considerable doubt upon some of the statements which Mrs. Dyson [had] ...

made in reference to the slightness of her intimacy with Peace'.[83] Clegg knew that it would be essential to push Katherine on both the authorship and content of these notes.

When Katherine failed, early in the cross-examination, to remember the date of her marriage to Mr Dyson, Clegg capitalised on this piece of luck and attempted to portray it as a sign of her lack of interest in her unhappy marriage, 'Don't you remember the date?'[84]

'No.'

'What year was it?'

'I can't tell you.'

'Please … listen to me. Do you mean to tell me, upon your oath, you cannot tell me what year you were married in?'

'I cannot tell the year … I can find out.'

'I want to know now. Do you mean to stand there and say you don't know what year you were married in?'

'No, I don't.'

'Where were you married?'

'I was married at the Trinity Church, Cleveland, Ohio.'

'Were there any witnesses present at your marriage?'

'Certainly.'

'What were their names?'

'My sister, Mrs Thomas Mooney.'

'Her Christian name?'

'Eliza.'

Mr Pollard objected to these questions about Mrs Dyson's wedding. 'Has the year when she was married,' he asked, 'anything to do with the question as to whether her husband was shot?' In response the magistrate expressed a hope that Mr Clegg would not proceed with this particular line of questioning much longer, but he allowed him to continue for the present:

'Mrs Mooney was one witness; who was the other?'

'Dr Sergeant.'

'Did you get a certificate of your marriage?'

'Certainly.'

'Did you bring that to England with you?'

'No; it is with my agents.'

'With your agents?'

'Yes.'

'What are your agents' names?'

'Barratt and Co.'

'Where is their place?'

'St Louis, Missouri, United States.'

'Had you any object in leaving your certificate there?'

'I have left the papers there because it is more safe than carrying them about.'

At this point the justice intervened to ask, 'Is there really any necessity for going into these particulars?'

Clegg explained his motive:

> I am bound to say at once this is a question of credibility as to what actually happened, and as this witness is the only person who actually tells us what happened I think I have a right to test her credibility in every possible way. That is my object in asking these questions.

He also said that he had a legitimate reason for asking about her marriage because of something that he had been told about it. This was a reference to the claim that Peace had been making that the Dysons were not married at all.[85] Clegg was permitted to continue, 'Was your husband friendly with the prisoner?'

'Yes, at first.'

'Did the prisoner frame any pictures for you?'

'Yes.'

Peace said something that was inaudible to all but those right beside him; Clegg carried on regardless, 'Can you tell me what they were?'

'Yes.'

'Please tell me.'

'There was a portrait of my sister, one of Mr Dyson, my brother, and my little boy.'

'Anybody else?'

'There were two taken from *Harper's Weekly*.'

'Your husband had a portrait picture of his mother?'

'There was one. I had one.'

Once more Mr Pollard queried the relevancy of the questions, but Clegg was again permitted to continue, 'Will you tell me when Peace framed the picture of your husband's mother?'

'No, he did not frame the picture, because that was in a pot frame which I bought, and what he did were in gilt frames.' Katherine admitted that she had discussed with him the possibility of framing photographs of both Arthur's mother and her own mother, but they were never done.

Again the magistrate asked Clegg why he wanted to know about all these 'extraneous matters'. To which he replied, 'If you want me to do so I will tell you what my object is; but I don't want the witness to hear. I have an object in view, and it is a material object, a most material object.'

He continued, 'Did you ever ask him to frame this portrait?'

'I mentioned to him about framing it, but I never got a photograph.'

'You had asked him to frame your husband's mother's portrait?'

'Yes, but he never did it.'

Clegg felt that the time was now right for him to move on to the question of those incriminating handwritten notes.

23

The Notes and the Ring

On the question of the notes found in the field and purported to have been written by Katherine Dyson to her lover Charles Peace, Clegg got straight to the point, 'Did you write him any letter?'

Katherine replied, 'No.'

Mr Clegg then took some paper from the batch of notes left on the table and handed it to Katherine, 'Now, is that your handwriting?'[86]

'No.'

'Keep them in your hand. Is it your husband's writing?'

'No.'

'Do you know whose writing it is?'

'No. I do not.'

'Did any person know of your wish for him to frame this picture of your husband's mother besides you and him and your husband?'

'Not that I am aware of.'

'Not that you are aware of. Have you ever seen the prisoner write?'

'No.'

'Will you swear you have never seen him write?'

'I never saw him write that I know of. I saw him with my husband whom he got … to write letters and receipts for him. I did not see him write, but I saw him sitting at the writing table with the writing materials before him.'

'Can you tell his writing if you see it?'

'I don't know. I did not see him write.'

'Have you never seen any letters that purported to come from him?'

'No.'

'You have not?'

'No. I don't know that he could write because he used to come and get Mr Dyson to write for him.'

'Then, so far as you are concerned, in reference to this wish that you wanted the prisoner to frame your photograph ...'

Mrs Dyson interrupted Clegg here. 'I did not ask him to frame my photograph.'

To which Clegg replied, rather testily, 'I did not say so; I said your husband's mother's photograph.' He continued with the cross-examination, 'You did not ask anybody [to frame the photograph]?'

'I don't think I did.'

He then asked Katherine to take the note and look at it. 'See that I read it correctly,' he said and began to read it out loud for the record:

Saturday Afternoon.

I write these few lines to thank you for all you kindness, which I shall never forget, from you and your wife. She is a good one. Does she know that you are to give me the things or not? How can you keep them concealed? One thing I wish you to do is to frame his mother's photograph and send it in with my music book. If you please, do it when he is in. Many thanks for your kind advice. I hope I shall benefit by it. I shall try to do right by everyone if I can, and shall always look upon you as a friend. Goodbye. I have not much time. Burn this when you have read it.

When he had finished reading the note that appeared to refer to framing the photograph of Mr Dyson's mother, he asked her directly, 'Now, Madam, will you venture to swear that that document is not in your writing?'

Her answer was definitive, 'No; it is not in my writing.'

At this point Peace interrupted the proceedings once again by moaning about the injustice of the inquiry. Mr Clegg, ignoring him, continued. He switched now to the issue of Peace and Katherine going out together socially, 'Now, Madam, remember you are on your oath.'

'I remember.'

'You were very intimate with the prisoner, were you not?'

'Yes, [I] used to go into his house with his wife and daughter.'

'Have not you and the prisoner, and without your husband and the prisoner's wife, been to a place of amusement?'

'I have been with him and his wife and his daughter.'

'I did not ask you that. I asked if you have been with him alone to places of amusement.'

'Not to places of amusement. I have called at one place in Sheffield with him alone.'

'What place?'

'I don't know where it is. The prisoner said there was a man there, and he called him his brother.'

'What sort of a place was it?'

'It was a public house.'

Mr Robinson, the assistant clerk, interjected to ask whether she had seen the man that the prisoner had called his brother, or not. She said she had. There were more inaudible moans from Peace before Clegg continued, 'Do you know the name of the street?'

'I don't.'

At this, Peace shouted out, 'Ask her about going to the theatre with me.'

Clegg obliged, 'Have you been to the theatre with the prisoner?'

'Yes, I have been with him and his wife and daughter.'

'Was your husband there?'

'No; I had other friends along with me.'

'Have you been to the Albert Hall alone with him?'

'To the Albert Hall? No. I was never with him alone at the Albert Hall. His daughter was with him.'

This answer caused Peace to straighten himself up and say, 'Send for Mr. Cowen, tailor.'

Clegg turned to him and said, 'Be quiet, will you? Have you, Mrs Dyson, and the prisoner, been in any public houses together?'

'I tell you we have been in one.'

'But more than once?'

'No; not alone with him. He has followed me into public houses when myself and my husband were together.'

'He has followed you into public houses?'

'Yes.'

'What house has he followed you in?'

'One at Darnall.'

'What is the name of it?'

'There were one or two of them. I cannot tell you the names.'

'Was one the Duke of York? Did you not go there alone?'

'Not me. I used to go there with my husband ...'

Clegg now tried to suggest that she had been buying alcohol and charging it to Peace's account. 'Did you not sometimes go to that house to get something to drink, and tell the landlord to put it down to Peace, the prisoner?'

'No. There was no landlord, only a landlady in the house, then.'

'Oh, do you remember that? The name is Mrs Liversidge, is it not? I ask you now, have you ever been to the Halfway House?'

'Yes.'

'Have you told the persons belonging to that house to put down the drink you had to Peace?'

'Not to my knowledge.'

'Not to your knowledge?'

'No.'

'Will you swear you have not?'

'I cannot swear it, but I say I never have to my knowledge.'

'Did you frequent that house?'

'I called there two or three times, I believe.'

'Did you know a person by the name of Goodlad?'

'Goodlad?'

'Yes, did you know the pianist at the Star Music Hall, in Spring Street?'

'No.'

Mr Goodlad was called in so that Katherine could take a look at him. She said that she could not remember having ever seen him before. Clegg persisted, 'Have you and the prisoner been to the Star Music Hall together?'

'I don't know it by that name.'

'Then I will ask you this question, have you been to a music hall together, and to a public house?'

'He called it a picture gallery. I did not hear any music there. There was not music there.'

'Where was it?'

'It was in Sheffield.'

'Can you tell me whereabouts it was?'

'I could not tell you the street. I could not find it now ...'

'Have you been to a music hall held at a public house, where there was some music and singing?'

'Not to my knowledge.'

'What?'

'It looked as if there was some music because there was a small stage, but there was no music in our time. It was early in the afternoon.'

'Have you not been at night when there have been music and singing, and that man who was called [i.e. Mr Goodlad] has been playing there?'

'No, I do not remember to have seen his face.'

'Do you know a public-house in Russell Street, Sheffield, called the Marquis of Waterford?'

'No. The public-house I am talking about now is in the street where the prisoner's brother lived.'

Katherine's answers could be seen as being highly evasive and not accommodating when they referred to any socialising she might have enjoyed with Peace and she made Mr Clegg work quite hard to get the responses that he wanted. He persevered, 'Have you been to more than one public-house with him?'

'I have been to the picture gallery and another place with him.'

'Those are two, and have you been with him to the Halfway House?'

'Not with him.'

'Or to the Duke of York's?'

'Not with him.'

'Have you and he been out of the town together?'

'Yes, he followed me one day to Mansfield.'

The questioning continued, but all Katherine would admit to was having had soda water with Peace in a public house, but not to having been to a music hall with him alone. Mr Clegg asked whether she had had a quarrel with the prisoner. She said that she had, that he was a nuisance and was 'running after' her. At this point, Peace lay his head on his hands, which were resting on the table.

As Katherine was questioned further about when they had had a quarrel, Peace was heard to say, 'Let me go away now; let me lie down; I cannot bear it'. Mr Hallam, the police surgeon, became concerned about his health and walked up to him and took his pulse. The surgeon declared that he was fit to remain where he was, but he was permitted to put his feet on a chair and seat himself in a more 'recumbent position'.

Clegg now wanted to return to the topic of the handwritten notes. Katherine Dyson, for her part, remained adamant that she knew nothing about these documents and that they were forgeries either written by Peace himself or by someone else on his behalf. Clegg asked her about the milkman who was alleged to have brought many of these notes between her and Peace, 'Do you know a person named Kirkham, a milkman, who used to deliver milk to you?'

'Yes, I know a milkman.'

'You know the man who used to deliver milk to you?'

'Yes; I should know him if I saw him.'

Mr Kirkham was brought in and Katherine duly identified him as her milkman. He was then led away again and Clegg asked Katherine if she had ever given him notes with instructions to deliver them to Mr Peace.

'I gave him two receipts that Mr Dyson had written out for him for pictures that he framed.'

'What were they in?'

'They were written on paper.'

'In an envelope?'

'I cannot remember whether they were in an envelope or addressed on a piece of paper. No, they were not in an envelope.'

'Have you not given him notes – not receipts?'

'Not notes; I have given him two receipts, I say.'

'I ask you, have you not given him notes?'

'No; not notes.'

'Little scraps of paper?'

'I gave him two receipts.'

'Where did your husband keep his address cards?'

'In his writing desk.'

'Locked up?'

'No.'

'Where was the writing desk?'

'In the sitting room.'

'Had you any address cards?'

'No.'

'Did you ever use your husband's?'

'No.'

One of the notes was then produced in court. It was written on one of Arthur Dyson's address cards, but a letter 's' had been added in pen to 'Mr Dyson' to make it 'Mrs Dyson'. The note read: 'After he is going out. I won't go out if I can help it. So see me.' In an apparent reference to Peace's daughter it ended, 'Love to Janey'. Clegg put it to Katherine, 'Will you venture to swear that you did not write that?'

Again, she was resolute, 'I did not write it.'

Clegg pointed out that the printing on the card had been altered, and he put it to her that she had added the letter 's' to change it from 'Mr' to 'Mrs'. She denied having done that. Clegg moved on to ask Katherine if she had ever given notes to a little girl called Hutton, the child of a neighbour in Darnall, to deliver to the prisoner, 'Now, didn't you use to give notes to this little girl? Will you swear that you never gave notes to the little girl to give to the prisoner?'

'I will swear it.'

Clegg decided to make a dramatic attempt to put Katherine under more pressure. He gave her a pen and some paper and asked her to write the words, 'I will write you a note when I can. Perhaps tomorrow.' When she had finished, he took the paper from her and, with consummate dramatic effect, held up the two pieces of paper in order to compare her handwriting with one of the notes held in evidence. He then asked her to write some more, 'You can give me something as a keepsake if you like but I don't want to be covetous and take them from your wife and daughter. Love to all.'

When she was finished, he again examined her handwriting, and then said to her, 'You have not written the last half so well as you did at the beginning'. She told him that it was the best she could do. Clegg then asked her to compare what she had just written with the handwriting on the notes found near the murder scene. 'Now, look at the first line on that card I have read to you. You still swear that is not your handwriting?'

'That is not my handwriting.'

'You will still swear it?'

'I say it is not my writing.'

'You still swear it upon your oath that that is not your writing?'

'I say that is not my writing.'

'Will you swear it?'

'I say it is not my writing.'

The magistrate grew impatient with Mr Clegg. 'You cannot have that too often,' he said.

Clegg persisted with the question while Katherine prevaricated, 'Will you swear that is not your writing?'

'I say it is not my writing.'

Peace was growing impatient as well. 'Make her swear it,' he shouted out. Clegg explained to the magistrate that he was persisting with the question because she was using the word 'say' and not 'swear'. Mr Pollard, for the defence, pointed out that this was not necessary as she was already under oath.

Having impressed the point as clearly as he could, Clegg had to move on. He came next to the reference in one of the notes to the gift of a ring, 'Did the prisoner ever give you a ring?'

'Yes; he gave me a ring.'

'He did?'

'Yes.'

'And did you write acknowledging the receipt of that ring?'

'Not to my knowledge ...'

She was handed a small envelope from the evidence, and Clegg asked, 'Had you any envelopes in your possession like that small envelope, with writing on it?' She attempted to look inside the envelope. 'Never mind the writing ... Had you any envelopes in your possession like that?'

'I cannot say.'

'It is very important.'

'I cannot say ...'

'... Was the prisoner living next door but one to you when he gave you that ring?'

'Yes.'

Everyone's attention was then draw momentarily to Peace as he was given some medication and moaned, 'I can't swallow it; I can't swallow it'.

When he quietened down, Clegg continued with his questions. 'Now, just look at that envelope ... Is that your writing?'

'No; it is not my writing.'

'It is not yours?'

'No.'

'Did anybody besides you and the prisoner know that he had given you the ring?'

'I don't know. I guess his daughter knew – at least he said so; but I don't know.'

'Do you know whether his daughter can write or not?'

'I don't know; I guess she could.'

'Do you know … when that ring was given to you?'

'No, I cannot remember.'

'You cannot tell?'

'No.'

'Can you give me any idea about what time it was?'

'No.'

'How soon was it before you left Darnall?'

'I say I do not know.'

'Was it before you had that portrait taken or afterwards?'

'I cannot tell you.'

'No idea?'

'No, I cannot tell you that.'

'You cannot give me any idea when it was?'

'No, I cannot.'

'Now, then, listen to me, follow me if you can, and tell me if I read too fast for you.' He then proceeded to read the specific note out loud:

I don't know what train we shall go by, for I have a good deal to do this morning. Will see you as soon as I possibly can. I think it will be easier when you leave. He won't watch so. The r--g [i.e. ring] fits the little finger. Many thanks. Love to Janey. I will tell you what I think of, when I see you, about arranging matters … Excuse the scribble …

Clegg then showed Katherine the note and, perhaps trying to get her to make a slip, asked, 'What is that other word there?'

'I don't know.'

'Just look please.'

'I cannot tell you.'

Katherine said the ring that Peace gave her had 'a few small glass stones in it', but she was adamant that this note about putting the ring on and it fitting was an absolute forgery. In fact, she said, it never did fit her and she did not keep it very long.

Mr Pollard objected, 'The witness keeps on saying she did not write the … notes. I object that unless it is proved the thing is connected with the case it cannot be used. She denies that she wrote it.'

Clegg disagreed, 'I submit, then, sir, that you have a most curious coincidence. She admits that the ring is given to her by the prisoner, and yet she denies writing the letter in which this very ring is mentioned to him.'

The magistrate, too, had decided that it was time to bring this particular line of questioning to an end. The potential impact of these notes was so important to Clegg that this suggestion led to quite a serious legal row between him and the magistrate:

Magistrate: 'What does it all lead to?'

Clegg: 'It leads to this. This woman has sworn now, as she did previously, that she did not write any of those letters, and I am in a position to prove that she did.'

Magistrate: 'She distinctly denies it. I did not, however, stop you when you said you would draw her attention to it, but I say that there is no necessity for going into the whole of it … You have quite enough to damage her credibility … I think enough has been gone into for the purposes of the preliminary examination. You can reserve the rest for the trial.'

Clegg: 'Supposing that at the trial this man is not defended, a state of things which is not at all unlikely.'

Magistrate: 'You know very well that in that case the judge would order some learned counsel to defend the prisoner. I am not going to deal with a state of circumstances that may arise at the trial. It would be presumption in me to provide for want of justice before the judges; it would be great presumption on my part.'

Clegg then tried a different argument, 'This is a preliminary inquiry, and I can put in whatever I think is for the benefit of the prisoner. Though it is only a preliminary inquiry, I am bound to do it.'

The magistrate was not convinced, 'I rule that sufficient has been asked about those letters'.

Clegg still objected and stated that he would have to be officially stopped by the magistrate in order for him to desist from this line of questioning. The magistrate complied, 'Then I stop you now. You have proved quite enough to indict her for perjury. That is all it can lead to. You can indict her for perjury if she has spoken falsely.'

Then Peace chipped in, 'You can do more than that.'

Clegg: '… at present I don't think I have got sufficient, in my opinion, to test this witness's credibility.'

Magistrate: 'In my opinion you have. If what you have asserted is shown to be true, you have more than sufficient to damage her credibility, and more than sufficient to have a cause for indicting her for perjury. Beyond that it is not necessary for you to go, and I rule that you shall not go.'

Clegg: 'How can I indict the woman for perjury unless I put the letters in her hands? I have the right to call for those to be read, and if you will not now let me cross-examine her in reference to them in detail, I ask that the letters be read; then I can cross-examine upon them, and that comes to the same thing.'

Magistrate: 'You should have done that before. It is too late now. I cannot have them read now.' The stipendiary magistrate was losing patience, 'You will take the ruling of the Court, Mr Clegg, if you please, and have done with it. You will take the ruling of the Court.'

Clegg: 'I put it to you as a matter of law.'

Magistrate: 'I have given my decision, Mr Clegg. You will please proceed with the case.'

Clegg: 'I object to proceed until these letters are read.'

Magistrate: 'You can proceed with your cross-examination.'

Clegg: 'I will proceed with my cross-examination if you let me go on as I have done.'

Magistrate: 'No, no; as to doing that, the time is past.'

Clegg: 'The time is not past, I submit, until the case is closed. It is not closed, and I have a right to have the letters read if I please.'

Clegg's persistence and audacity suddenly reaped reward. The magistrate agreed, 'You can read them over yourself if you like.'

Clegg: 'If they are put into my hands I shall read them to [the] witness.'

Magistrate: 'Then you may read them.'

Clegg regarded this as a victory. 'Very well, sir,' he said, 'then that is all I want.' He then turned his attention back to Katherine, 'Have you read them?'

'Some of them.'

'Have you read them all?'

'Not all of them.'

'Then I will read them to you.' Clegg read another of the notes: 'If you have a note for me, send now, whilst he is out; but you must not venture, for he is watching, and you cannot be too careful. I went to Sheffield yesterday, but I could not see you anywhere. Were you out? Love to Jane.'

Once again, Katherine denied that she was the author of this note. She also denied, when it was put to her, that she had ever given Peace an American cent coin. Clegg went on reading from the notes and getting Katherine to transcribe pieces from them, while she continued to deny having anything to do with them. There was, at times, an element of farce about it all as, throughout this debate about the handwritten notes, there were intermittent interruptions from Peace; he gave shouts of 'hear, hear' in support of Mr Clegg at times, and at other times complained loudly about the grave injustice that was being done to him.

In the end Clegg had to leave the matter of the notes and move on. He next probed the question of whether Katherine was ever really afraid of Charles Peace. 'What do you ... say,' he asked her, 'was the reason for your leaving Darnall?'

She replied, 'Because we were afraid of him. That was the reason.' She also spoke of the threatening letters that purported to have come from Peace in Germany, which, she explained, her husband had handed over to their solicitor.

Clegg asked Katherine about her version of the events as they had occurred on the night of Mr Dyson's death. She denied that when she found Peace waiting for her in their yard that night she had said, 'You old devil, what are you doing here now? I should have thought you had brought enough disgrace upon me?' She told the court that she did not remember saying anything at all to him.

According to Katherine, Peace did not say, 'I have come to try and see you, and get your husband to come to terms, as I am away from my wife'. Nor did he say, 'I will let you have the notes back again if you will get him to stay proceedings'. All she remembered him saying was, 'Speak, or I'll fire'. Katherine was adamant that no struggle of any kind had taken place between the two men that night and, in fact, her husband never spoke to Peace at all. She was sure that Peace never said, 'If you don't stop I'll fire', before he shot Arthur. According to her, he simply shot her husband who 'dropped instantly'. Clegg's cross-examination of Katherine Dyson came to an end.

24

'Base, Bad Woman'

Mr William Clegg had made a robust attempt to attribute blame to Katherine Dyson and to discredit her by focussing so much upon the handwritten notes and her alleged intimate relationship with Peace. Yet the comments that she had made about her own and her husband's fear of Peace, and their desire to be free of him, seemed to resonate with those listening and with the newspaper reporters. A correspondent for *The Times* noted her comments on the matter the next day:

> She left Darnall because the prisoner annoyed her. They were afraid of him. They were afraid he would come to them in the night. They were told by the neighbours that he used to visit Darnall at night in female attire … the prisoner threatened her husband's life, as well as her own, prior to their removal. He said he would blow her brains out and those of her husband also … At the time they removed the prisoner had made himself very disagreeable and annoying, but her husband would not quarrel. He would not speak to the prisoner.

Police Constable Pearson was called to give evidence at the preliminary hearing and he told of his vain efforts, as instructed by the chief constable, Mr Jackson, to find Charles Peace after Mr Dyson's death. Mr Pollard wanted to introduce evidence of what he called the prisoner's recent attempt to escape from the train. He argued that 'if Peace had been an innocent man he would not have made an attempt to get away'. His request to introduce this as evidence was denied.

The hearing of evidence for the prosecution was now at an end. It was Mr Clegg's professional opinion that it would not benefit his client's case to call any witnesses, but Peace disagreed. 'Cannot you call my witnesses?' Peace asked. 'What is the use of my having witnesses if they are not called?' The magistrate told him that, first of all, the charge had to be read to him and then he could make a statement. He could also call witnesses at that time if he so wished.

The charge was read by the magistrate and Peace was asked if he had anything to say in response. 'If you take my advice,' Clegg told him before he could answer, 'you will simply say not guilty.' Peace did say 'not guilty', but then ignored his counsel's advice by saying more:

> ... justice has not been done to me. I can prove that I am not guilty. That is what I want. I want that. I want justice done to me. Why don't they let me call my witnesses? Can my witnesses be called upon my trial and me not pay the expenses. Can they be at my trial if I cannot pay their expenses?

The magistrate asked him to clarify exactly what he was unhappy about. 'I want my witnesses to be called to prove I have really not done this,' he said. He went on to assert that Katherine had threatened him with a pistol and had threatened her own husband's life as well. He called her a 'base, bad woman'. 'You are not taking your trial today,' the magistrate reminded him. 'This is only a preliminary inquiry. Are there any witnesses or not?' Mr Clegg told him that he had no witnesses to call.

It cannot have surprised many people when the magistrate came to the determination that Peace should be committed to appear on trial at the assizes in Leeds the following week. Clegg had done his best for him. He had done all he could to discredit Katherine's reputation and suggest that there was an illicit affair behind the dispute between Peace and the Dysons. Perhaps he had succeeded in making some people doubtful about Katherine's moral character, but without achieving much success in ameliorating the outcome for his client.

Clegg's own opinion, expressed many years later, was that Katherine Dyson was 'one of the cleverest women witnesses' that he ever encountered in court. In his opinion she was not being honest about her relationship with Peace and she was the real author of those personal notes written to him. '... just as I was getting to the serious point,' Clegg wrote, 'she fell back on the well-known trick of witnesses who have got into difficulties – loss of memory.'[87]

Clegg had regarded Peace's preliminary hearing as being important enough to be late for a crucial football match. The story goes that Clegg, an England international in his spare time, arrived late for England's match against Wales on Saturday, 18 January 1879, played at the Kennington Oval. It was the first time that the two teams had played an international match against each other and because of his attendance at Peace's inquiry, Clegg could not catch the train from Sheffield to London on the Friday evening. The following morning the weather was atrocious and heavy snow delayed his train. It is said that England began the match with ten men until he arrived twenty minutes late. The weather was so bad, and the pitch so heavily covered with snow, that the teams agreed to play only thirty minutes a side. At least Clegg's difficult journey south was rewarded with a 2–1 victory for England.

Before he was removed from the corridor that had served as a makeshift courtroom, Peace complained that he was cold and asked Mr Clegg if he could sit in front of the fire for a little while before being brought back to his cell. The first thought of many people was that he was going to attempt another escape. Sensing the way the authorities were thinking, Peace suggested that they put him in irons when they did this. If he did indeed have any plans to escape, the prison surgeon scuppered them by determining that Peace's cell would be quite warm enough for him.

Even though the hearing had been held in private at the alternative venue, the press coverage meant that the public were kept well informed of events. The story of Charles Peace and Mrs Dyson was proving to be of great fascination. 'The greatest excitement prevailed in the town during the hearing of the case, and both stations were crowded with people, who watched the London and Leeds trains in the hope of seeing Peace.'[88]

Peace spent that night in his cold cell at the police station. The following morning he was visited by the police surgeon and certified fit to be moved.[89] As soon as word spread that the prison van was being prepared, crowds of people began to gather. A mattress and rugs were placed in the van before Peace was carried out. He appeared in his convict uniform, looking 'pale and haggard' with a large white bandage wrapped around his head.[90] Many were surprised that he was not manacled or handcuffed for the journey.[91]

He was driven to Midland Station where many more people waited to catch sight of him. Although the officers in charge tried to elude the crowd by bypassing the passenger entrance and driving straight to 'a siding far beyond the booking offices', the people were not to be denied their fun and ran after them. The mattress and rugs were put in an uncoupled passenger guard's van into which the prisoner was then transferred. It was reported that Constable Robinson was there and had a brief conversation with Peace.[92] When the 2.12 train to Wakefield arrived at the station the carriage containing Peace was pushed from the siding and coupled to it. The crowd watched as the train departed the station.

On 29 January 1879, Peace was transported from Wakefield Prison to Armley Gaol in Leeds to await his trial for murder.[93] By then great improvements in his health were reported and, as *The Times* put it, he had 'almost recovered from the effects of the wound he sustained in attempting to escape'.[94]

In order to avoid any incidents, and to counteract the growing public interest in his case, the timetable for his removal from Wakefield had been kept a strict secret. Even Peace did not know when he was to be transported until he was given the order in his cell to get ready.[95] His transportation party to Armley Gaol was heavily armed; three armed warders travelled with him in a cab, while four more followed behind in another carriage. The party arrived at Armley Gaol at 3.15 p.m.[96]

In a few days' time Peace would finally stand trial for the murder of Arthur Dyson. He knew that if he was to mount a serious legal challenge to save his life he would need money to get witnesses and build a case. With this in mind he had written to the women in his life for assistance. His letter to Sue was dated 26 January 1879:

My dear Sue

This is a fearful affair which has befallen me, but I hope you will not forsake me, as you have been my bosom friend, and you have oftimes said you loved me, and would die for me. What I hope and trust you will do is to sell the goods I left with you to raise money to engage a barrister for me, to save me from the perjury of that villainous woman, Mrs. Dyson. It will have to be done at once, and the money you send let it go to Clegg and Sons, 57 Bank Street, Sheffield. You must do it with all speed … I hope you will not forget the love we have had for each other. Do your best for me. I should like you to write or come and see me if you could. I am very ill from the effects of the jump from the train. I tried to kill myself to skip all further trouble and distress, and to be buried at Darnall – I remain your ever true lover till death.[97]

He wrote to his wife, Hannah, on 29 January 1879:

Dear wife and children,

I am still very ill, and think I shall be no better in this world. You say in your letter that the people will not come forward and speak for me. I always told you to summon them, and not to ask them at all; and when they had once been in court the Treasury would have paid their expenses and compelled them to be at the assizes free of all expense to you. But now you have involved this expense on yourself, I think; but you must do your best for me …

… I have also wrote to transfer all property to Mr. Clegg. Order him to have the property in London sold for my defence and to prosecute any persons who are in possession of it …

… you had better go and see Mr. Clegg to see if he is taking any steps to have this property sold …

I now conclude with my best love to all dear friends. I remain your affectionate and unhappy husband …

In the end, neither of the women was willing nor able to give him much financial assistance.

The Banner Cross Murder Trial

On 30 January 1879, the last remaining formality standing between Peace and his trial for murder was traversed when the grand jury returned a true bill against him for the murder of Arthur Dyson. His trial was scheduled to take place on Tuesday, 4 February 1879 in Leeds. This time, if found guilty, he would be sentenced to death.

Appointed to handle his prosecution were Mr Thomas Campbell Foster and Mr Hugh Shield. He was defended by Mr Frank Lockwood and Mr Stuart-Wortley, and two of Peace's prized violins were sold to help pay for his defence.[98] Lockwood was a competent courtroom advocate who would later be elected as a Member of Parliament and be appointed to the position of Solicitor General. He was described as having 'a handsome presence, a fresh, frank, open countenance, a beautiful voice and a charming manner'.[99] Regarded by his colleagues at the bar as a dangerous opponent and 'a dextrous cross-examiner', he would need every quality he possessed if he was to save Charles Peace from the gallows.[100] He also had a talent for illustration and often made drawings, usually humorous, of scenes and characters from the trials in which he was a participant. His sketch of Charles Peace sitting in the dock during his trial is a good example of this.

The presiding judge for the case was Mr Justice Lopes who had attempted, as head of the Manchester grand jury, to get the bill against the Habron brothers for the murder of Constable Cock thrown out. Later he would be appointed lord justice and raised to the title of Baron Ludlow. Sitting alongside him on the bench for this high profile case were a number of dignitaries including the high sheriff and the lord mayor.

Peace was led into court not looking in his best physical condition. He was, according to one reporter, 'a shabby, wretched-looking old man, looking as if hope had left him; grey hair, closely cropped; cheeks hollow; lips pale'. Mentally, though,

Frank Lockwood's drawing of his client Charles Peace sitting in court. (Topfoto)

he seemed as quick as ever with 'eyes steely, keen, and restlessly watchful'.[101] When asked to plead to the charge of wilful murder, he answered, 'Not guilty'.

In his opening statement to the jury Mr Campbell Foster, for the Crown prosecution, acknowledged that the case had been 'so much commented on by the Press and by the public that it would be a difficult matter for a jury to enter upon the inquiry as though the matter were now for the first time brought to them'.[102] Nevertheless, he implored them to be fair in their judgement:

> … To put from your minds – to put entirely out of your consideration, if you
> can – anything that you may have read about this case, and be guided entirely by
> the sworn testimony to be given before you to-day in arriving at a judgement as
> to the guilt or innocence of the prisoner.[103]

He then went on to outline the details of the case leading up to death of Mr Dyson and the events of the night of the shooting itself from the point of view of the prosecution. Peace's legal counsel, Mr Lockwood, remained quiet until Mr Thomas Campbell Foster began to tell the jury about Peace's recent jump from the train. 'I don't know, my Lord,' he said, 'how far my friend is justified in introducing this matter as part of his case. It is not a matter affecting the guilt or innocence of the accused.'[104] Justice Lopes agreed with him and Campbell Foster was forced to move on.

A surveyor from Sheffield called Mr Johnson was the first witness called to the stand. He gave evidence regarding the plan of the Dysons' house and the area around it. He also said that he had known Mr Dyson personally and described him as 'a tall muscular man, though perhaps a little delicate'.[105]

The main witness for the prosecution was, of course, Katherine Dyson and she found herself back in a witness box once again, this time examined first by Hugh Shield on behalf of the Crown. Just as she had at the preliminary hearing in Sheffield before the magistrate, she outlined how she and her husband had first become involved with Charles Peace, how he had come to live near them in Darnall and had framed a number of pictures for her and her husband. She told the court how, at first, he had been welcome to call at their house, but then Mr Dyson grew to dislike him and asked him to stop. She explained how he had become a nuisance and would not leave them alone and how Arthur Dyson had thrown the card into Peace's garden asking him to stop interfering with them. That card was produced in court and she identified her husband's writing on it.

Katherine went on to describe the escalation in the tension that had developed between themselves and Peace, including his attempted tripping up of her husband in the street and his threat, in front of witnesses, to blow her brains out. She told the court how they had even gone to the extent of having a summons taken out against him, for which Peace had failed to appear, and how a warrant had consequently been issued for his arrest. She was asked to describe the events of the night of 29 November 1876 and her husband's death, which she did.

As everyone in court was aware of how dramatic and putative Mrs Dyson's last cross-examination had been when conducted by Mr Clegg at the preliminary hearing, her cross-examination at the trial was expected to be a highlight. Mr Lockwood took on the job of conducting it himself and he began in dramatic form by telling Mrs Dyson that he would be some time and, if she so wished, she could sit down. Perhaps in a show of defiance or determination, she opted to remain standing.[106]

Under Lockwood's cross-examination Katherine continued to deny the idea that any physical struggle had taken place between her husband and Peace that night. She said that although her husband may have wanted to grab hold of Mr Peace, he had not succeeded in doing so. Lockwood tried hard to suggest to the jury that the shooting was the result of a desperate fight between the two men, 'Did anything touch him before he [i.e. Mr Dyson] fell?'[107]

'No.'

'Will you swear that?'

'The bullet touched him, of course.'

'I did not ask you that. Did this man [pointing to Peace] touch him with his fist?'

'No, the bullet touched him.'

'After the first shot was fired, will you swear your husband did not come up and take hold of this man?'

'He did not take hold of him.'

'Did he not catch hold of him by the arm?'

'No.'

'Wait a moment. Did he not catch hold of him by the arm which held the revolver?'

'No.'

'And did not Peace strike your husband in the face with his fist about the chin and nose?'

'No.'

'Will you swear that your husband was not touched in the face by him?'

'He was not touched in the face by him; it was by the bullet.'

Lockwood tried to identify Katherine's relationship with Peace as a source of conflict between the two men. At one point he just asked her directly whether her husband was jealous of them, to which she replied, 'No'. She said that her husband first objected to Peace's behaviour around the spring of 1876.

When questioned about the photograph of herself and Peace at Sheffield Fair, at first she said that it had been taken in the summer of 1875. Mr Lockwood then put it to her that she had not met Peace for the first time until November of 1875. The implication was that the photograph was taken at the Sheffield Summer Fair of 1876, after her husband had made it clear that he did not like Peace and wanted them to have no more to do with him.

'How comes it, Mrs Dyson,' Lockwood asked her, 'that you were at that fair being photographed with the man with whose conduct your husband was dissatisfied in the spring of that year?'

It was obvious to those in court that this suggestion perturbed her somewhat. 'I think there is a mistake in the dates, sir,' she replied. She attempted to explain the confusion away by saying that 'she was not sure about dates … She had been travelling, and had been knocked about a good deal and [had] forgotten dates.'

The handwritten notes that had been found in the field across the road from the Dysons' house, and had caused such controversy at the inquiry before the stipendiary magistrate, were raised again. Lockwood questioned Katherine about them and asked her to examine the handwriting in some of them. Just as she had before, she denied categorically that she had anything to do with them.[108] Lockwood asked her to write in court, which she did 'very calmly', asking for permission to blot when finished.[109] He asked her about the milkman and the little girl whom, it was alleged, she had used to carry these notes to and from Mr Peace. She continued to insist that the only paper she ever sent Peace was in the form of receipts for pictures that he had framed for customers and her husband had written out for him. As she had done at the preliminary hearing, Katherine admitted that she had accepted a ring from Peace, but said that she had thrown it away soon afterwards because it was too small and 'not worth keeping'.[110]

Katherine was again put under pressure about the exact nature of her relationship with Peace and the extent of the socialising in which they had engaged together. She admitted to being once, or perhaps twice, in Peace's company at the Marquis of Waterford public house and once at the Star Music Hall. She said that 'to her knowledge' she had never requested that drink consumed by her at the Halfway House Inn at Darnall be charged to Peace's account.

In response to Lockwood's claim that she had been 'turned out' of the Halfway House as a result of being drunk, she said that she only remembered being 'slightly inebriated' and had no memory of being 'turned out'. She said that she had told her husband about being out with Peace on one occasion and, admittedly, 'he did not like it'. She did not tell him that they had been to a public house, but told him instead that they had gone to a picture gallery as the place to which they had been was both a public house and a picture gallery.[111] She admitting going to a number of other places with Peace but always, she claimed, in the company of either her little son, Mrs Padmore's little boy or some other child.[112]

Lockwood put it to her that she was in the Stag Hotel at Sharrow on the day before her husband's death, in the company of Mrs Padmore's little boy, and that a man had come over and sat down beside her. That man then followed her outside. His contention was that the man in question was Charles Peace. She admitted that a man did speak to her that day, but she could not remember if she had replied to him or not. She said that she 'was almost ready to swear' that the man in question was not Mr Peace. When interrogated for using the phrase 'almost ready to swear' rather than just 'swear', she put her slight uncertainty down to Peace's ability to disguise himself. She said that the man she saw on that day appeared to her to be only 25 years of age. She denied Lockwood's assertion that the man had said to her that he would come and see her the next night.

Under cross-examination, Katherine once again did her best to minimise the significance of her relationship with Peace and refute the claim that she had written the incriminating notes, but her claims not to remember certain dates correctly and particular meetings with Peace were not entirely convincing. Nevertheless, when Katherine's period in the witness box finally came to an end, most agreed that she had equipped herself quite well. Once again, under intense questioning, she had held up and her answers had come across as mostly emphatic and consistent. Although many may have believed that she did indeed have some sort of illicit romantic relationship with Charles Peace, this did not seem to take away from the credibility of her evidence about what had happened on the night of her husband's death.

I Will Have My Turn

The prosecution called a number of witnesses who claimed to have either seen Peace in the vicinity of the Dysons' house on the night of the shooting, or had heard screams and shots. Mary Ann Gregory, the grocer's wife from Banner Cross, told her story about meeting Peace at their shop on the night of the murder. She also described the horrible scene that she had witnessed at the Dysons' house a little later, 'I saw several people and they appeared to be carrying one man. I could not distinctly see who they were, but they carried Mr. Dyson into his house, and I there found him sitting in a chair. He was insensible and blood was streaming down his face.'[113]

Mrs Sarah Colgreaves gave evidence about her meeting with Peace that night and his use of offensive language to her regarding Mrs Dyson. Charles Brassington too, the witness who Peace claimed had perjured himself at the preliminary hearing, was called to testify before the jury in Leeds. Once again his evidence was that around eight o'clock on the night Arthur Dyson was murdered, a man with whom he was not acquainted came up to him and engaged him in conversation outside the Banner Cross Hotel, only a few yards from the Dysons' home. Brassington told the court about the letters and the photographs that the man wanted him to look at and how he had been disparaging and threatening about the Dysons. Brassington said that that he was standing under a gas lamp and it was a bright moonlit night. He swore that the accused in the dock was the same man that he spoke to that night and any amount of questioning from Mr Lockwood on the matter could not shake his conviction.

A quarryman named Charles Wyman told the court that on the night in question he was in the Banner Cross Hotel. At around eight o'clock he heard two gunshots. He went to the door of the hotel and heard Mrs Dyson screaming. He ran to their house and saw 'Mr. Dyson lying on the floor and Mrs. Dyson holding his head'.[114]

Thomas Wilson, the 17-year-old scythe maker, also told of hearing the shots and seeing a man cross the road and climb over a wall on the other side of the road. Like Wyman, he went to the Dysons' house and saw the injured Arthur Dyson that night.[115] As Wilson was leaving the witness box, Peace shouted at him, 'You villain!'[116]

Mr James William Harrison, the surgeon, gave evidence once again about how he had tended to the wounded Mr Dyson on the night in question. He informed the court that the patient had died around ten o'clock. Mr Harrison testified that he found the wound in Mr Dyson's temple to be very deep and extending upwards obliquely.[117] He was quite clear that 'the bullet in the brain was the cause of death'.[118] He removed the bullet, he said, and gave it to Police Inspector David Bradbury. He noted that there were also 'slight' abrasions on Mr Dyson's chin and nose. Mr Lockwood wanted these abrasions interpreted as the result of a violent struggle that had taken place between Peace and Dyson. Under cross-examination from Lockwood, however, Harrison refused to accept the idea that the abrasions were the result of receiving the blow of a fist to the face. He was adamant that they could not be, even if the person striking such a blow was wearing a ring at the time. They were, in his professional opinion, the result of Mr Dyson's fall after being shot.

The police inspector, David Bradbury, produced the bullet that had been given to him by the surgeon. He also had a photograph that depicted two people. Mrs Dyson was recalled to the stand briefly and she identified the photograph to be the one of herself and Peace at Sheffield Fair.[119] Police Constable George Ward told the court that he had conducted a search in the vicinity of the crime scene and in the field opposite Gregory's house where he had found the bundle of handwritten notes.

Evidence was also presented regarding the threats made by Peace against the Dysons in Darnall in July 1876. The neighbour, Rose Annie Sykes, testified that she had been living next door to the Dysons in Darnall at that time and she witnessed Peace making threats against them, including the incident when he took out a revolver and threatened to blow their brains out. She also said that she had never seen Katherine inebriated. Contrary to claims made by Peace that Katherine had hit him with a life preserver at some time, she said that she had never seen her hit Peace or anyone else. Jim Sykes corroborated his wife's evidence and on hearing him do so, Peace shouted out, 'You bloody villain, I will have my turn yet; you are a devil!'[120] Mrs Padmore, who was also present on the street that night in Darnall, was also called to testify and she agreed with the evidence given by Mrs Sykes.

Constable Edward Robinson and Sergeant Charles Brown testified regarding Peace's violent arrest at Blackheath in October 1878. The revolver that they had taken from Peace that night was produced in court. Expert evidence was given by Mr Woodward, a gun and rifle maker from St James' Street, London; he said that the rifling of the bullet taken from Mr Dyson's head was consistent with those fired at Constable Robinson from Peace's revolver in Blackheath.[121] That brought the case for the prosecution to a close and Mr Lockwood said that he had no witnesses to call for the defence.

A Cry for Blood

Mr Thomas Campbell Foster, in his closing statement for the prosecution, said, 'The object of the cross-examination of Mrs Dyson had evidently been to throw doubt upon her evidence and to prejudice the jury against her'. In his view 'her testimony remained unshaken'.[122] He put it to the jury that if Mr Lockwood had been attempting to prove 'improper intimacy' on the part of Mrs Dyson with the prisoner, 'had not those attempts signally and miserably failed?'[123] Campbell Foster questioned this strategy because, as he saw it, even if the defence counsel had succeeded in having such aspersions accepted, then 'would it not have suggested that there might have been jealousy on the part of the prisoner, and was not jealousy the passion that more than any other prompted men to the commission of desperate deeds?'[124] He posed the essential question for the jury, 'Even if Mrs Dyson and Peace had been intimate in the way which had been suggested, was that any justification for taking the life of Mr Dyson?'[125]

Campbell Foster paid a somewhat insincere compliment to the acting abilities of his adversary, Mr Lockwood, while in the process dismissing his cross-examination of Mrs Dyson as a sham:

> … though the jury might not have detected it, it was a charming piece of acting, an art in which there was no one more accomplished than … [my] learned friend. It was a solemn sham, employed for producing a bad impression, and acted simply for the purpose of throwing dust in the eyes of the jury.[126]

He rejected completely the idea of a struggle having taken place between Mr Dyson and the prisoner:

It certainly had been hinted at that there was a struggle between the deceased and the prisoner; but where was the evidence of it? ... There certainly had been no such struggle; but the prisoner's advisers had not anything better to put forward by way of defence.[127]

Campbell Foster argued that 'although many imputations had been cast upon Mrs Dyson' her evidence had been 'at every step ... plainly and strongly corroborated'.[128] He put it to the jury, therefore, that the circumstantial evidence was so convincing in this case that they 'ought to have no difficulty in concluding that this shooting had been done by Peace with malicious intent'.[129]

When it was the turn of Mr Lockwood to make his final attempt at saving the life of his infamous client, he began his closing statement by informing the jury of how seriously he took the responsibility. 'I don't think any man in any profession has a more painful duty, or a more onerous duty to discharge, than when he feels he has to stand as it were alone against the whole world to protect the life of his fellow-man.'[130] He decried the sensationalist interest that there had been in this case. 'From one end of this country to the other,' he said, 'there has been a wild and merciless cry for blood, which is a disgrace to the country in which I now stand.'[131] He placed a large portion of the blame for that 'cry for blood' on the nature of the coverage that the newspapers had given the case:

Never in the whole course of my experience – and I defy any of my learned friends sitting around me to quote an experience to the contrary – has there been such an attempt made on the part of those who should be the most careful of all to preserve the liberties of their fellow-men ... to determine the guilt of a man.[132]

Lockwood was blunt about the motivation of these newspapers, 'They have not hesitated for a moment, for the sake of the paltry pence which they could snatch from the public, which they wickedly tried to gull, to prejudice this man's life'. He said all this to supporting exclamations of 'hear, hear!' from Peace.

Lockwood probed and reminded the gentlemen of the jury about the necessity for them to be impartial in their consideration of the case. He acknowledged how difficult that might be:

Can I hope for a moment that when this question had been discussed and canvassed, aye, and determined, throughout the length and breadth of this country, you have not been drawn into the cortex of that discussion? ... You have had your ears filled with reports; and you with others, actuated by what you have read, have discussed this matter, and possibly – I don't know whether it

Frank Lockwood made the final attempt in his closing statement to save the life of Charles Peace. (Topfoto)

is so or not – possibly you have come into the box today with a strong opinion formed as to the merits of this case.[133]

He challenged them to remain detached from all that they had heard outside of the courtroom and try the case fairly on what they had heard inside:

Won't you be careful when you come to consider your verdict? Won't you be careful to see that any such bias, if it does exist, has been thoroughly eliminated? Oh, gentlemen, I implore you by all you hold most sacred, dismiss from your mind any such feeling as that.[134]

Lockwood reminded the jury members that the responsibility of proving guilt in the case lay, as always, with the prosecution. He accepted that perhaps the prisoner had led a wicked life but, he argued, that was why they had to be careful about sending him to his death. 'You must remember,' he told them, 'that if his life has been a wicked one, he, of all others, is least fitted to be hurried into the presence of his God, where he will be judged again.' This may have been a somewhat bizarre line of argument to use in a plea for leniency, but Peace seemed to appreciate it. 'I am not fit to die!' he shouted out.[135]

Lockwood referred back to Mr Thomas Campbell Foster's jibe about him 'acting' when he cross-examined Mrs Dyson and the description of his line of defence as a 'sham':

[He] … called what I have done a piece of acting. He told you that what I had attempted was a solemn farce. That in cross-examining Mrs. Dyson I was only carrying out that which in his opinion was a mere piece of acting, which he was clever enough to see through. Gentlemen, I grant my learned friend great credit. Experience and age always bring their fruits. But was my learned friend acting?[136]

His opponent, he said, had tried to misrepresent the defence argument:

He put it to you that perhaps I was going to set before you a case that, if this man had carried on an intrigue with that woman, it gave him the right to shoot her husband! But, gentlemen, you know perfectly well that that was never the defence I was going to put before you on behalf of this man.[137]

Lockwood told them that his aim, in his questions to Mrs Dyson, had been to expose her lack of credibility. That was his duty, he explained, because she was the only witness 'who could speak to what occurred in the passage outside her house'.[138] Her credibility was an important issue, 'When you have got one witness standing alone, speaking as to a transaction, it surely becomes a material thing to inquire as to how far you may rely upon her testimony'.[139]

In his view, Katherine Dyson was an unreliable witness. Her evidence was, he asserted, 'beyond all doubt contradicted in many material points'.[140] He urged the gentlemen of the jury to view that evidence 'with very great suspicion'.[141] He pointed to a number of inconsistencies and contradictions in her story.

For example, he said, there was that photograph of her and Peace taken at Sheffield Summer Fair. He reminded them again that as she had not met Peace for the first time until November 1875, the photograph must have been taken in the summer of 1876. That was at the time her husband was actively trying to distance them from Peace. So this meant, Lockwood said, 'after the time her husband had become dissatisfied, she was keeping up a communication with this man … she was going about with this man, and she was being photographed with him'.[142] He also criticised Katherine for the occasions during cross-examination when she had failed to answer his questions directly and when she had refused to swear definitively about going with Peace to public houses and the like.

Lockwood contended that, contrary to what Katherine had said, the death of Mr Dyson was the result of an accident, nothing more. He proposed that the most likely scenario was that a struggle had taken place between these two men that night over Katherine Dyson's affections, and Arthur Dyson had been shot accidentally. 'If that were so,' he said, 'then the crime was not one of murder.'[143] It was perfectly clear to him that the first shot fired by Peace that night was intended to frighten Mr Dyson as he was about to engage Peace in a physical struggle:

> … the weapon might have been discharged for the purpose of frightening Dyson. It should be remembered as a point in the prisoner's favour that the bullet was found high up in the wall; a shot fired … would hardly have been found there if it had not been fired for the purpose of frightening him.[144]

According to Lockwood's version of events, the warning shot failed to deter Dyson and the men began to fight:

> … this big man Dyson pursued the prisoner for the purpose of seizing, and, as I suggest now to you, actually did seize him. A struggle had taken place; in the course of it the revolver, which was in the hand of this man, might have gone off. It might easily have done so, and had death been so caused, that clearly was not murder.[145]

Lockwood reminded the jury that he had pressed Mrs Dyson on this issue of a struggle having taken place between the two men and he found her answers to be unconvincing.[146] Why, he asked the gentlemen of the jury, if Mr Dyson was walking straight down the passageway after the prisoner, as Mrs Dyson had claimed, did the bullet enter at the temple rather than 'through the front of the head'?

> Does that look as if the prisoner fired at Mr. Dyson as he was calmly and slowly coming down the passage, or did it look as if the pistol had been discharged during a struggle – when the prisoner's hand was aloft and an attempt was being made to wrest the weapon from his grasp?[147]

The evidence of the surgeon, Mr Harrison, did nothing to dissuade Lockwood of the contention that it was an accidental shooting. After all, he pointed out, even the upwards momentum of the fatal bullet was consistent with the idea of a struggle going on between the two men at that moment:

> Did not all this show that at the time a struggle was going on; that the hand of one of the men was being held and pressed towards the head of the man who was holding him; and that when the struggle was going on the pistol went off.[148]

Mr Harrison may have stated that in his opinion the abrasion on Mr Dyson's face was not the result of a fight, but Lockwood disagreed. The prosecution, he said, wanted to use the surgeon's evidence to claim that the abrasion was caused by the deceased banging his face when he fell, but they did not have 'a tittle of evidence on which to test the theory'.[149] Lockwood told the jury members that they would have to decide about this. 'It ... was not a question of medical skill or of scientific opinion,' he told them, 'it is a question for you as men of common sense to say whether the abrasion could have been caused by a blow on the face.'[150]

He urged the jury not to place any store in the threats allegedly made by his client against the Dysons, such as those stated by the witnesses Mr Brassington, Rose Annie Sykes and others. He knew, he said, that his client was 'a wild and reckless man', prone to making idle threats.[151] 'It would be quite possible for such a man as that,' he said, 'to use threats under the influence of passion which he did not really intend to carry out.'[152]

In conclusion, Lockwood asked the jury to bring in a verdict of acquittal on the charge of murder as 'the prosecution had failed by means of satisfactory testimony and reliable witnesses to bring the charge home to the prisoner at the bar'.[153]

28

Justice and Jury

'I earnestly implore you', Mr Justice Lopes asked the gentlemen of jury before they left to make their decision, 'to discard from your minds everything you may have heard or read about the case before you came into Court.'[154] He, like Mr Lockwood, was critical of the newspaper coverage of the case and he told the gentlemen of the jury that they must come to a verdict determined only by a consideration of evidence as it had been presented in court. They would have to decide, Lopes told them, whether Mr Dyson's death was the result of wilful murder, or if some lesser charge such as manslaughter was more appropriate. If they believed the version of events put forward by Mr Lockwood, wherein the killing was the result of two men engaging in 'an angry scuffle', then manslaughter would be the correct verdict and not murder.

He described this scenario for them:

> … the first shot was fired simply to frighten either Mr. or Mrs. Dyson; … then a scuffle ensued between Mr. Dyson and the prisoner; and … in the course of this scuffle the pistol, which the prisoner was carrying, accidentally went off and thus accidentally caused the death of Mr. Dyson.[155]

For this version to be true, he told them, they would have to disbelieve the testimony of Mrs Dyson 'because there can be no question that, if you accept her evidence as true, the theory of the defence … falls to the ground'.[156]

Mr Justice Lopes told them that he, personally, was not convinced by the theory. 'I am bound to say,' he told the jury, 'it is very much a theory with but little, if any, evidence in support of it.'[157] He referred to the fact that Mr Lockwood, as was his duty, had attempted to discredit Mrs Dyson over the course of his lengthy cross-examination of her. Mr Lockwood complained that she had contradicted herself on a number of occasions, had been unclear about certain facts and had been hesitant about answering certain questions.

Mr Justice Lopes reminded them that, although Mr Lockwood had questioned Mrs Dyson's degree of intimacy with the prisoner, they must put aside any prejudice they might have formed regarding 'improper familiarity' between her and the prisoner. Mr Lockwood, he said, had been perfectly justified in his attempts to discredit her evidence in this way but, importantly, many aspects of the case did not rest on her evidence alone. For example, he told them, Mrs Dyson's testimony regarding the threats made by Peace in July 1878 was corroborated by three other witnesses. Also, he said, it is not denied by anyone 'that the prisoner was there [or] that shots were fired'.[158]

This notion of 'the accidental discharge' of the prisoner's pistol was 'the most important ingredient' in the defence scenario. In the opinion of Mr Justice Lopes, however, there was no evidence for it. He described it as nothing less than 'an absolute inference; an absolute surmise'.[159] He even asked each of the gentlemen of the jury in turn to take the pistol into their own hands, to try the trigger, and see if they thought it could go off accidentally.

When he had concluded his statement, Mr Justice Lopes told them that it was now time for them to decide:

> The case now passes from me to you. You have a most responsible duty to discharge. You are bound to look carefully into the whole of the evidence; if you can conscientiously give the prisoner the benefit of any doubt you ought to give it to him. On the other hand, if the evidence is such as to satisfy you that the prisoner did commit this murder, and that here was no solid ground on which the defence could rest, then you must recollect that you own a duty to the community at large, and must also recollect the duty you have incurred by the oath you have taken.[160]

It was 7.13 p.m. when the jury members retired to consider their verdict. It took only twelve minutes for them to return. The clerk of the arraigns asked the foreman of the jury if they had agreed upon the verdict and he confirmed that they had. The foreman announced that they found the prisoner guilty.

Peace was asked if he had anything to say in response to the verdict. For someone who had plenty to say during the trial, perhaps it is surprising that his only answer at this time was, 'It is no use my saying anything'.[161] Justice Lopes then addressed him directly:

> Charles Peace, after a most patient trial, and after every argument has been urged by your learned counsel on your behalf which ingenuity could suggest, you have

been found guilty of the murder of Arthur Dyson by a jury of your countrymen.
It is not my duty, still less is it my desire, to aggravate your feelings at this moment
by a recapitulation of any portion of the details of what, I fear, I can only call
your criminal career. I implore you during the short time that may remain you
to live to prepare for eternity.[162]

He donned the black cap and proceeded to pass sentence:

I pass upon you that sentence, the only sentence, which the law permits in a
case of this kind. That sentence is that you be taken from this place to the place
whence you came, and thence to a place of execution, and that you be there
hanged by the neck until you are dead, and that your body be afterwards buried
in the precincts of the gaol wherein you were last confined before the execution
of this judgement upon you. And may the Lord have mercy upon your soul.[163]

The condemned man seemed to accept his fate with composure and resignation. It
was reported that as he was being walked to the prison van for transportation back
to Armley Gaol, Peace turned to one of the officials to make a comment, 'Well,
I'm a-going to be executed, and I suppose I can't complain, but what I say is this:
I'm going to be hung for what I done, but never intended'.[164]

It is safe to say that most people did not agree with him. Although many
suspected that Katherine Dyson had not acted like an angel, they still believed that
Peace's killing of Arthur Dyson was murder:

... whether his [i.e. Peace's] own account of his relations with Mrs. Dyson,
or her account, or the third and most probable theory, that she was a foolish
woman of a vulgar type, who accepted attentions from vanity and was concealing
something in her evidence, but not much, is the true one, does not signify a jot.
If the evidence is true, Peace resolved to shoot Dyson whenever Dyson's jealousy
became inconvenient, and did shoot him, and if that is not murder, there is no
such crime.[165]

Part 4

Rewards and other Matters

Susan Gray, or 'Mrs Thompson', had received the letter from Peace, just before his trial, in which he had asked her for much needed financial help and expressed his undying love for her. The truth was that by this time Sue knew that Peace was unlikely to gain his freedom again and she was trying desperately to distance herself from him. It is clear from her reply to his plea for help that her main aim now was to look after herself:

> I received your letter and am truly sorry to receive one from you from a prison, and in regard to what you ask me I have parted with all the things in my possession. I sold some of the goods before Hannah and I went away and I shared with her the money that was in the house, and what I had, had to be sold for my subsistence as you well know. I had nothing to depend upon, and have not a friend of my own, but what have turned their backs upon me, my life is indeed most miserable.

Sue was very anxious that Peace stop telling everyone how close they were and, even worse, how she had assisted him in his criminal work:

> You are doing me a great injury by saying I have been out to work with you. Do not die with such a base falsehood upon your conscience, for you know I am young and have my home and character to redeem. I pity you and myself to think we should have met. In conclusion, I hope and trust you will be very penitent and that we shall meet in Heaven.

Sue had another reason to distance herself from Peace; on 5 February 1879, the day after Peace had been sentenced to death for the murder of Arthur Dyson, she applied to the Treasury for the £100 reward that had been on offer for information leading to his capture. She sent her application to Mr Pollard and received the following reply, dated 6 February 1879, from Mr Stephenson, the solicitor to the Treasury:

> Madam,
> Your letter addressed to Mr. Pollard, of this department, asking for the Government reward in this case – £100 for such information as would lead to the conviction, &c. – has been handed to me.
>   I have no authority to deal with your application, which should be made to the Home Office.[1]

She took Mr Stephenson's advice and wrote directly to the Home Secretary, Mr Assheton Cross, at Whitehall, on 11 March:

> I hereby beg to make formal application for the reward ... offered on the conviction of Charles F. Peace. The information was given by me to inspectors Bonny & Philips of the R Division on Nov. 5 1878, in the presence of Mr. & Mrs. Brion. The Treasury have instructed me to make this claim to your dept.
>   Awaiting your favourable consideration ...[2]

It is interesting that she signed the letter 'Bailey alias Thompson' and then asked in a postscript that they address the reply to the name 'Mrs Daly'. She explained the reason was because 'I do not want to be known. I have suffered so much.'[3]

Obviously Sue was a woman with many secrets. She has been criticised for attempting to claim the reward, an action that could be interpreted as a betrayal of her former lover.[4] There is a distinct possibility, however, that Peace might have found the claim amusing. For her, as his lover, to claim the reward money from the authorities in that way would take, surely, the kind of audacity he would admire.

Peace knew that Sue had not really tried to help him financially in his time of need. 'She [i.e. Sue] says she has nothing to make money off for me,' he wrote in a letter to Hannah, 'I know she has plenty of things to make money off for me.'[5] Yet, despite Sue's refusal to assist him financially and her efforts to publicly distance herself from him, it is clear that Peace still had a great deal of affection for her. He wrote asking her to visit him in prison and she was willing to do so:

You have expressed a wish to see me. I shall come down to Leeds to know if
I can be admitted, and, if possible, to cheer you up a little. You know what we
have been to each other – all in all – until this has befallen you and me who has
suffered so greatly. – Darling.
Yours, Sue.[6]

In the end, though, Peace's family were against Sue coming to visit him in prison.
His official request for the visit was granted initially but later denied, perhaps at
the request of his family. Although he dearly wanted to see Sue, in the end he
complied with the wishes of his family. That did not prevent him from sending
her affectionate letters to the end: 'I hope you will be prosperous in the world. My
poor, poor Sue. O do forgive me for the trouble and the blows I have given you.
God bless both of us.'[7]

Mr Brion was another applicant for the £100 reward. He claimed that he
had helped in the identification of Peace and had given information on the
whereabouts of some of the stolen property. He had been aware, for example, that
some of Peace's property was stored at Petticoat Lane. According to him, he had
been so taken in by Peace that he had assisted him innocently. In fact, he said, even
after Peace's arrest he was having a hard time accepting the truth about his friend.
Brion had taken Peace to be a religious man and made that clear in a letter written
after the conviction for murder:

I never thought that you were an irreligious man, and even now I believe that
had you early confided in a sound, Christian friend you would have left your
evil ways ... You remember that on Sunday evenings you used to enjoy singing
hymns of praise. Notwithstanding all that has been revealed of your life, I really
believe that you did enjoy those hymns, and therefore believe that there is hope.
Even those hymns may have been heard in Heaven, and be remembered there
now to your good.[8]

The popular suspicion regarding Mr Brion, of course, was that he was so close
to Peace that he must have known about the criminal activities. Probably in
response to a request from Brion, Peace wrote him a letter in which he stated
clearly that his friend and fellow inventor never knew anything about his
criminal activities:

... it will give me great pleasure to speak the truth in this matter ... I do say
truly that neither you nor any friend or neighbour within miles of Nunhead or
Peckham Rye did know anything of what I was doing ... I always represented
myself as an independent man, and also was very careful about going out and
coming in, so that I know there was no suspicion on me. As for you, Mr. Brion,

you might have lived in my house along with me and I should not have let you know anything. So that I am very sorry to think that people round Peckham Rye should so most wrongfully affect an innocent man's character by connecting it with one of the worst men that this world ever produced.[9]

He also drew up a document granting his rights in three of their inventions to Mr Brion:

To Mr. Henry F. Brion, 22, Philip Road, Peckham Rye.
H.M. Prison, Leeds, February 20th, 1879.

I, Charles Peace, freely and without cost, herewith of my own accord, give to Mr. Henry Brion my inventions as follows:

1   Invention for supplying members of fire-brigades and other with pure air when buildings are on fire.
2   Improved brush for washing railway-carriages, etc.
3   Hydraulic tank for supply of water.

He signed it and had the prison chaplain witness it.

From his prison cell Peace was still proclaiming his innocence. He did not deny that he had shot and killed Arthur Dyson, but he did not accept that he had committed wilful murder. The killing of Arthur Dyson, he maintained, was 'unintentional'; it was the result of a violent struggle. He insisted that had he really intended to kill Dyson that night, he would have done so in a much more secretive and devious manner:

I did not kill Mr. Dyson intentionally, and I most solemnly swear that in shooting at him I did not intend to murder him. If anyone thinks for a moment he will see that I never intended murder when I went to Banner Cross. If I had meant to murder Mr. and Mrs. Dyson, or either of them, I knew the place well enough. All I had got to do was to go to the door, walk in, and shoot them both as they were sitting.[10]

Peace claimed that he even thought about going back to help Mr Dyson as he made his getaway, but by that time people had begun to gather and he was 'greatly agitated'. He opted to run instead.

He contradicted the accounts given by a number of witnesses in court, especially those who said that he had made threats against Katherine Dyson. According to him they were all lying, 'I call God to witness that I never threatened Mrs Dyson. Mrs Dyson and I were on such intimate terms that it would not have suited my purpose to have done so.'[11] He only went to Banner Cross that night, he said, to have the warrant revoked. 'I was tired of being hunted …,' he said. 'If I had got that warrant withdrawn I should then have gone away.'

Listening to Peace you would have thought that he was being very reasonable about it all that night and that the Dysons were the aggressors. 'Mrs Dyson became very noisy,' he said, 'and used fearful language and threats against me, and I got angry.' Before long Mr Dyson arrived on the scene. Peace would have everyone believe that he just wanted to get away, but Arthur Dyson would not let him:

> As soon as I saw him I immediately started down the passage which leads to the main road. Before I could do so, Mr. Dyson seized me. … we struggled together, and he seemed likely to get the better of me. He had got hold of the arm to which I had strapped my revolver, and then I knew I had not a moment to spare … It was a life-and-death struggle.[12]

Peace continued to tell his version of events, but no one was listening anymore. The newspapers reported that, for a time, Peace was refusing to eat and drink.[13] They speculated that his wish may be to commit suicide and in order to prevent this nine warders were assigned to stay in his cell, three at a time in eight-hour shifts.[14] It was reported soon afterwards that he had begun to eat normally again.[15]

Peace would soon be led to the gallows but, before that, he had one more big shock in store for the custodians of British justice.

The Incredible Confession of 'a Hardened Wretch'

The eventful life of Charles Peace was coming near to its end, but he still had a secret to reveal and it concerned no small matter. We must turn our attention back nearly three years to early August 1876, and the murder of young Police Constable Nicholas Cock in Manchester.

The day before he killed Arthur Dyson, Peace had attended the trial at which the 18-year-old William Habron was found guilty of Constable Cock's murder and sentenced to death. One day in February 1879, from his cell at Armley Gaol, Peace asked to see the governor, saying that he had a confession to make. He caused amazement by telling the governor that it was he who had shot and killed Constable Cock at Whalley Range that night in 1876. He claimed that the young man who had been convicted of the crime, i.e. William Habron, was completely innocent.

Ever since the conviction of William Habron, there had been considerable controversy over the verdict. Many people were unimpressed by the flimsy evidence that had led to the young Irishman's conviction. The footprint found near the murder scene, they argued, which had been relied on so heavily by Superintendent Bent and the Crown prosecution, was far from satisfactory evidence. Even if that print had been made by William's left boot, and this was in doubt since no impression or photograph was ever produced in court, it only proved that William was there at some time and did not prove that he was present at the actual murder.

There was also dissatisfaction with the testimony given by Mr McClelland in which he claimed that William Habron had visited the ironmongers only hours before the murder to inquire about buying ammunition and a revolver. Those who opposed the verdict said that there was no satisfactory proof that the man in question was William Habron. Mr McClelland said it was Habron, but his fellow shop worker could not be sure.

The evidence of William Habron's co-workers at Deakin's Nursery, if believed, made it impossible for him to be there because he was at work all that day. In any event, said the dissenters, even if it was William Habron who spoke to Mr McClelland that day, it only proved that he looked at ammunition and not that he actually bought any; he did not buy anything from Mr McClelland.

The mysterious man seen near the murder scene that night by Constable Beanland, John Massey Simpson and the deceased Constable Cock was not proven to be William Habron either. The man they saw was described by Massey Simpson as being a much older man. Even if William Habron was seen around there that night, it did not prove that he killed Constable Cock; after all, he lived nearby.

The motivation of revenge proposed by the prosecution was also questioned. It was true that Constable Cock had arrested and charged the Habrons on a minor offence, and they had gone around the place making verbose threats against his well-being. Those who objected to the verdict said, however, that this was not sufficient motivation for Habron to kill Cock. Many other people in the area were fed up with the constable's diligence as well, but they were not accused of killing him. The fact that William Habron vocalised such annoyance did not prove that he went out that night and committed murder. It was also true that the Habron brothers seemed to be well regarded by those who knew them and not known as particularly violent people. The threats they made were said by many to have been nothing more than idle talk.

Luckily for William Habron, there had been much public disquiet about his conviction and death sentence. Even Justice Lindley, who had presided over the case, admitted that he was not happy with the conviction.[16]

Eight thousand people had signed a petition asking the Home Secretary to grant Habron a reprieve from execution at the very least.[17] John Habron, who was back in Ireland at the time, wrote a letter of thanks to a Mr Megson of Manchester who was one of the main instigators of the petition. John began by reiterating his own and William's innocence. '[I] am glad to say,' he wrote, 'that either me or my brother William … never had anything to do with that dastardly crime.'[18] He was, he wrote, very grateful for what Mr Megson and the others had done on their behalf and he hoped that someday in the future full retribution could be achieved for his brother:

> Mr. Megson, I feel and ought to be, and am very much obliged to you and all the other gentlemen who did so befriend … William after his sentence.
>
> … It's a very poor and hard case to us his brothers and parents, knowing the man innocent … but I hope the lord will show justice some day and whoever

has done the dastardly crime, I hope will be found yet … I am certain if not for you gentlemen who looked after him after his sentence he would have suffered wrong, for which we fell very thankful. But as you gentlemen did so well for him, I hope you will try and perhaps help to get him out of misery in time to come.[19]

John Habron also told Mr Megson about the severe financial stress that the case had brought on his family, 'I am very sorry we have lost all our hard earnings by trying to defend ourselves. It cost us about £150, so by money we can do no more.'

The efforts of those trying to help the Habrons paid off only just in time when, two days prior to the date appointed for his hanging, William was granted a reprieve from execution by the Home Secretary on the grounds that 'the evidence was not sufficient to justify the verdict'.[20] His sentence was commuted to penal servitude for life. The official line at the time was that, although they believed him to be involved in the murder, they could not be sure that he had actually fired the shot that killed Cock.[21] William remained a prisoner but was at least alive. It was still hard for him to accept, and when a fellow prisoner went to the gallows on the same day that had been scheduled for his own execution, the quiet young Irishman could not help but reveal his thoughts to his priest, 'Well, it is all over for him and would have been all over for me, too. Now I shall perhaps be in prison all the days of my life, but as long as I live I shall always pray they will find the man who killed Cock.'[22]

Now, finally, there was hope. Charles Peace's confession to the Whalley Range murder, if true, proved that Superintendent Bent had been misguided in his belief about the guilt of William Habron and a terrible miscarriage of British justice had taken place. By now William was in the third year of his life sentence; he had spent eight months picking oakum at Millbank Prison, followed by a move to Portland Prison where he was engaged in even more strenuous physical work at the stone quarries.[23]

Peace's claim was sensational. He said that he had been out on his usual rampage of house theft that night in the rich neighbourhood of Whalley Range. Although he saw two policemen chatting on the road, he decided to continue to his target destination anyway. He was intent on robbing the property of Mr Gratrix that night, but once inside the garden he heard a step coming behind him. 'Looking back,' he said, 'I saw it was one of the policemen I had passed on the road.'[24] That policeman was Constable Beanland.

Determined to get away, Peace jumped over the garden wall back out onto the road which, unfortunately, brought him face to face with the diminutive Constable Cock. 'I all but fell into the arms of a second policeman,' he said, 'who must have been planted for me.' Cock made an attempt to arrest him but, said Peace, 'My blood was up being nettled that I had been disturbed'.[25]

He pulled a revolver on Constable Cock and warned him to stand back. Being the determined character that he was, Cock refused to back down, with the result that Peace fired two shots at him. The first went wide of the target but the second hit Cock in the body causing the fatal wound. Peace then made his escape, leaving Constable Cock badly wounded. He climbed over walls, crossed fields and eventually made his way to Old Trafford railway station.[26] He did not board a train there, but walked instead through the tunnel and along the railway track for around 2 miles before eventually joining the road.

As he made his escape that night, Peace said that he came upon a man sitting near a fire, but the man did not see him.[27] Peace disappeared into the night; his presence in the area of Whalley Range was not known and he was never even a suspect in the case. Instead, Superintendent Bent and the police became obsessed with achieving the conviction of those they thought responsible for the crime, namely the Habron brothers.

When Peace heard about the trial of the Habrons he decided to attend and, of course, the following day murdered Arthur Dyson. It is almost as if in the aftermath of William Habron's conviction for Cock's murder, Peace had become increasingly emboldened by his ability to avoid justice. Perhaps he became caught up by the euphoric fantasy of being able to get away with anything, including murder.

The problem for the authorities was that Peace was a thief, a murderer and an inveterate liar. Was he telling the truth? Was he just looking for attention, or trying to delay his own execution, or hoping to get leniency? Was he just trifling with the authorities? Many were sceptical:

> Any remorse that Peace may have felt about the matter must have been of nicely graduated weakness, since it induced him to confess his guilt when the confession could not possibly do him any harm, although it had been quite inoperative at the time when Habron's life was in imminent danger.[28]

To prove that he was telling the truth, Peace drew up a plan of the place where Constable Cock had been shot and gave detailed information on what had taken place that night. He said that he wanted to officially confess the crime to his former vicar from Darnall, Reverend J. H. Littlewood, and he wrote to him requesting a visit:

> Dear Sir, –
> This is from that poor, miserable man, Charles Peace, now lying under sentence of death in prison … I have a great desire to see you as early as possible this week, if you don't think it too much trouble or think that I am so base and bad that it is not worth your while to see me. But, O sir, do come and see me at once, for

I have a great message for you to bear to the people of Darnall, and I think you yourself will not repent coming to see me.[29]

The vicar agreed, arriving on 19 February 1879, and Peace told him why he had sent for him. 'I wanted to see you to unburden my mind to you. I know I am about to die, and I want to take from my conscience some things which weigh heavily upon it.'[30]

He then confessed Constable Cock's murder to the clergyman and asked him to do whatever he could to get William Habron set free. He was adamant, just as he was about the murder of Arthur Dyson, that he had never intended to kill the constable:

Now, Sir, I want to tell you, and to make you believe me, when I say that I always made it a rule, during the whole course of my career, never to take life if I could avoid it. Whether you believe me or not, I never wanted to murder anybody, and only wanted to do what I came to do and to get away; and it does seem odd, after all, that in the end I should have to be hanged for having taken life – the very thing I was always so anxious to avoid. I have never willingly or knowingly hurt a living creature.[31]

He explained to the clergyman how it came about, then, that he wounded Constable Cock fatally on that night in 1876:

I fired wide at him; but the policeman was as determined a man as myself, and after I had fired wide at him – and it was all the work of a few moments … I saw I had no time to lose if I wanted to get away … I then fired the second time, but all I wanted to do then was to disable the man … in order that I might get away. I had no intention of killing him. We had a scuffle together. I could not take as careful an aim as I would have done, and the ball missing the arm, struck him in the breast, and he fell. I know no more. I got away, which was all I wanted.[32]

Peace explained why he had attended the trial of the Habron brothers:

I saw in the papers that certain men had been taken into custody for the murder of this policeman. That interested me. I liked to attend a trial, and I determined to be present … I attended the Manchester Assizes for two days.[33]

He attempted to excuse himself for allowing William Habron to face the hangman's noose for a crime that he had committed:

Now, Sir, some people will say that I was a hardened wretch for allowing an innocent man to suffer for my crime. But what man would have done otherwise in my position? Could I have done otherwise, knowing as I did that I should certainly be hanged for the crime?[34]

But now, he told Reverend Littlewood, it was different, 'now that I am going to forfeit my own life, and feel that I have nothing to gain by further secrecy, I think it right, in the sight of God and man, to clear the young man, who is innocent of the crime'.[35]

Having listened very carefully to Peace, Reverend Littlewood was convinced that he was telling the truth, 'I cannot conceive it possible that any human being in your fearful position could deliberately lie, and confirm these lies, knowing that your Creator and Judge is conscious of all you say, and that you will have to render an account of it all.'[36]

Peace also went on to confess Cock's murder to the chaplain of Armley Gaol, Reverend Osmond Cookson, and to anyone else who would listen.[37] He backed up his verbal confessions with a written statement, which the prison authorities forwarded to the Home Office for urgent attention. Again, just like an earlier letter written to the Home Office, Peace's spelling and grammar were idiosyncratic:

> There was tow brothers triad for the morder of Police man cox in Seymour Grove at Whalley range near Manchester ther was from seven to ten witnesses appeared against them & all of them but one perjered themselves against them to the uttermost. for I saw this trial myself [sic].[38]

Nevertheless, the document did contain a considerable amount of detail and even a plan of the crime scene drawn by Peace himself.[39] He was even able to supply the murder weapon, which Superintendent Bent and his men had been unable to do at the time of the Habron trial:

> ... you will find that the ball that was taken out of Cock's breast ... was fired out of my revolver, now at the Leeds Town Hall ... What I have said is nothing but the truth & this man is innocent. I have done my duty & the rest I leave up to you.[40]

Doubts about the veracity of Peace's confession persisted. Sceptics pointed to what seemed to be a number of errors in his account of what had happened.

Firstly, there were some problems with his map of the locality: he showed a hoarding that didn't exist, a mansion in the area, Manley Hall, was put on the wrong side of the road and the escape route allegedly taken by him would have brought him straight past Constable Beanland which, according to the constable himself, did not happen. Also, Peace said that on the night in question 'he saw a man sitting near an open fire near a large excavation'.[41]

Critics of his story said that although the man was there, he 'had also been there every night for months before' and so Peace could have seen him at any time.[42] Although Peace confirmed that his shot had hit the constable 'on the nipple', sceptics said that he could have read this in the newspapers or, in fact, heard it at the Habron trial. They also said that it was, as *The Times* reported it, 'utterly impossible that the murderer, whoever he was, could have stopped on the spot long enough to ascertain in what part of his body Cock was struck'.[43]

Other people pointed out that Peace, in his written statement, referred to John and William Habron as 'Frank and Aaron Harman'.[44] Constable Beanland, for his part, referred to the fact that in Peace's statement he said that he had struggled with Constable Cock; Beanland claimed that there was no time for a struggle to have taken place between the two men.[45] There was also a controversy about Peace making reference to Cock having drawn his police staff on him that night, whereas Cock's staff was actually still in its case in the constable's pocket when the others found him lying wounded.[46]

Those who believed Peace's story pointed out that most of the discrepancies in his account actually came from Reverend Littlewood's report of what Peace had said to him, rather than Peace's own written confession. It is true that Reverend Littlewood had quoted Peace as saying that a struggle had taken place between himself and Cock, but the prison chaplain, Reverend Osmond Cookson, to whom Peace had also confessed, said that this was Littlewood's mistake. To him Peace had 'said plainly that no scuffle whatever took place, and that Cock was shot before arriving at actual close quarters'.[47]

It is true that in Peace's own written account there is no mention of a physical struggle. Reverend Cookson also claimed that the confusion about whether Cock's staff was drawn or not came from a another misunderstanding on the part of Reverend Littlewood. To Cookson, Peace had never mentioned a staff; he had said that 'Cock was about to strike him on the head with a stick'.[48] Reverend Cookson believed that Reverend Littlewood 'jumped to the conclusion that as a staff is the weapon supplied to police men it was with such a weapon that Cock intended to strike Peace'.[49] Again, in his written confession, Peace mentions 'a walking stick' and not a police staff.[50] Cookson said that his version had been corroborated by two prison wardens, both of whom had heard Peace give his confession to Reverend Littlewood.

Many people were concerned about Peace's motivation for coming out and saying all this now. In Reverend Cookson's opinion, any suggestion that Peace was making the confession purely to delay his own execution was 'simply a fabrication'.[51] Mr Lockwood, who of course had defended Peace at this trial, was not convinced. He was consulted for his opinion on the matter and he took the side of those who were doubtful about Peace's confession. Being aware of Peace's capacity for deviousness, he said that 'he did not believe that Peace had anything whatever to do with the murder' and that it was an attempt 'by the convict to postpone the carrying out of the sentence'.[52]

Doubts were also expressed regarding the ballistics. It was argued that although Peace said that the fatal bullet was fired from a pin-fire revolver, which the experts said had no grooves in them, the one that killed Cock was grooved at one end.[53] But then Mr Woodward, the gun expert who had given evidence at the Banner Cross murder trial, made a dramatic and important intervention. He examined the bullets in question and was categorical in his judgement: 'The bullets taken respectively from Dyson's head and Cock's body, and the Blackheath bullet fired at Robinson … are from identically the same mould, and I am convinced all three bullets were fired from the pistol submitted for my experiments.'[54]

A committee of expert gunsmiths, including Mr Woodward, was convened by the Home Secretary at his official residence to investigate the matter. The experts were asked to look at Peace's revolver along with the bullets taken from the bodies of Cock and Dyson and the one extracted from the arm of Constable Robinson. The conclusion of the committee was clear: 'The committee came to the unanimous decision that the three extracted bullets were each of them fired from Peace's revolver.'[55]

Richard Owen, a renowned and controversial naturalist and biologist, was also asked for his opinion on the similarity between the bullet extracted from Cock's body and one that Mr Woodward had fired from Charles Peace's revolver; he said that they both came from a revolver of the same 'pattern'.[56]

Political pressure was now building regarding the unsoundness of William Habron's conviction; the Home Secretary, Richard Assheton Cross, was asked in the House of Commons on 27 February whether, in the light of Peace's confession, an inquiry into Habron's conviction would be instituted. A number of petitions calling for Habron's discharge were presented to both the Home Office and the House of Commons, in which were stated the problems with the original conviction:

> That the prosecution in Habron's case is disbelieved; that Habron calling at a
> shop in Oxford Road, Manchester, about some cartridges is entirely a mistake;
> that the caps in Habron's pocket prove nothing, inasmuch as his employer
> used caps occasionally and had given Habron his cast-off clothing, some caps
> having been left in the waistcoat, trousers, or coat; that Peace has confessed to
> having murdered P.C. Cock, as stated in the letter from the Rev. Mr. Cookson,
> chaplain of Armley Prison; that the bullet found in Cock's body is of the same

kind as those used by Peace; that Habron has always protested his innocence; that the summing-up of the judge who presided at the trial was in Habron's favour; and that the finding of the jury in Habron's case was not according to the weight of evidence.[57]

Notwithstanding the doubts many people had regarding Peace's integrity, the Home Office and the Home Secretary took his confession very seriously. Mr Assheton Cross told the House of Commons that it required 'most careful consideration' and 'must undergo the most careful scrutiny'.[58] An official inquiry into Habron's conviction was established.

A Wrong put Right

The inquiry into the conviction of William Habron re-examined all the evidence in the case and on 17 March the Home Secretary made an important statement to the House of Commons:

> When the confession was made by Peace, before his execution, I felt, of course, that it was quite necessary to consider very carefully the whole circumstances of the case again; and I stated to the House that, owing to that confession, it would receive the most anxious consideration of the Secretary of State as to how far the sentence should be allowed to stand … The result to which I certainly myself have come is that the statement made by the man Peace has been so entirely corroborated in many important points, that I shall feel it my duty to recommend the Crown to grant a free pardon to William Habron … in that conclusion I have the entire concurrence of the learned Judge who tried the case, and of the Law Officers of the Crown.[59]

So, finally William Habron was to be set free. The announcement was greeted with cheers from the members in the House of Commons. Although he knew it was unusual in such cases, Mr Assheton Cross thought it fitting that compensation should be considered so that 'the future of this unfortunate and unhappy man will be provided for'.[60] The end result was that William Habron was declared an innocent man and awarded £1,000 compensation.

Most people now accepted that the original verdict at the Habron trial had been a serious miscarriage of justice. The Home Secretary said in the House of Commons that he would be in favour of a change to the law in order to enable appeals on matter of fact in such cases in future, a right not available to those convicted in criminal cases at the time.[61]

Blame for the Habron miscarriage could be apportioned in a number of directions:

> ... [It] was a case of circumstantial evidence exclusively. Habron's threat directed at Constable Cock and the latter's murder immediately thereafter turned public suspicion naturally upon Habron. Whether Inspector Bent was altogether accurate in his report on the boots was later seriously doubted. The prosecution, convinced of Habron's guilt, discredited all the evidence pointing to his complete innocence. The jury were convinced by the prosecution's clever construction of its theory of guilt and fell into the same trap of blindness to the factors indicating innocence. But for Peace's insatiable appetite for crime, it is quite possible that Habron would have served out his life term. Peace's confession was ... a matter of good luck for Habron.[62]

Superintendent Bent, who had been so important in achieving the conviction, remained unconvinced. He lessened the importance of the circumstantial evidence at the trial and stated that the conviction had been achieved primarily as a result of the evidence given by witnesses called on behalf of the defence. He was referring, in particular, to the witnesses whose evidence conflicted with alleged earlier statements they had made to Inspector Henderson. He said that those witnesses were called at the demand of the Habrons, in opposition to their legal advice:

> ... against the wish of their counsel, the prisoners determined to call witnesses ... several witnesses were accordingly placed in the box for the defence, but on being cross-examined by Mr. Higgin, the *alibi* which they endeavoured to prove was shattered to pieces, their statements being very different from those which they had signed at the time the Habrons were before the magistrates. In fact, I believe it was their contradictory statements which caused William Habron to be convicted, more than any evidence given by the police or other persons who were examined for the prosecution.[63]

He also pointed to the fact that the Habrons themselves were responsible for the public threats that they had made against Constable Cock. Had they not made such threats, he claimed, they would not have been suspected or arrested in the first place.[64] He reminded people that it was not the police who proved that these threats had been made, it was those members of the public who gave evidence. He also dismissed any claims made that he had not investigated the crime adequately or that he had not pursued other lines of inquiry.

His critics accused him of assuming the guilt of the Habrons from the start of the investigation and, thereby, failing to accommodate other possibilities. He denied this. 'I was in duty bound to make every possible inquiry,' he said, 'which I did.'[65] According to Bent, none of the other possibilities that they looked at were credible. In the end, though, the superintendent had to accept the outcome, which he did with some degree of equanimity: 'I had no desire to see either him or any other person executed; and if the authorities were satisfied that he was not guilty, I had no right to be dissatisfied with the decision at which they had arrived.'[66]

Justice Lindley did not blame Bent or his men for what had happened. According to the Home Secretary, speaking in the House of Commons, Lindley thought that 'the evidence of the police was given with fairness and impartiality and an absence of zeal and eagerness'.[67]

The authorities, now extremely embarrassed by the whole episode, wanted to ensure that those hostile to them would not capitalise on William Habron's release from prison for propaganda purposes, so they endeavoured to manage it very carefully. A meeting was arranged between the Home Secretary and William Habron's former employer, Mr Deakin. Deakin was asked to meet the prisoner on the day of his release and make sure that he did 'not fall into the hands of agitators'.[68] The Home Secretary was aware that the infamy of the Habron case had already led to offers from a number of 'public entertainers' for William to appear in their shows.[69] Mr Deakin gave assurances that he would meet William and ensure that any such thing did not happen. It was also agreed that William Habron's compensation award would be invested for him, with the Catholic Bishop of Salford and Mr Deakin appointed as trustees.[70] Mr Deakin was authorised to pay for all of William Habron's expenses for travelling, clothes and the like, and to forward the bill to the Home Office.

Although William Habron was being held at Portland Prison it was decided not to release him from there directly, instead he was to be brought first to Millbank Prison in London. 'Prisoner C 1547', as he was known, got up as usual that morning at quarter past five to begin his day. William Habron had no idea of the momentous day that lay ahead. Soon the warders came for him, but they told him nothing of what was about to happen:

> They said never a word, but took me to the weighing room and weighed me, and walked me into the chief warder's hall, where they stripped me of my clothes, and gave me another suit. They then brought me outside the front gate to the governor's room, to undergo the doctor's examination, and answer his questions as to general health, and so forth. I answered him as well as I could, and then knew, from seeing two or three other prisoners, that we going to be moved to Portland. I supposed I looked a little surprised, for the chief warder asked me if

I did not know I was going away in the morning, and I answered him that I did not. Nor did I.[71]

During the journey to London, and despite the fact that the authorities were aware that William had been granted his freedom, he was forced to travel in handcuffs. He arrived with the other prisoners into Vauxhall Station in London from where he was transported to Millbank Prison. His memories of the prison were not wholly negative and when he arrived there he was welcomed with some warmth. 'When I got to Millbank in a cab from Vauxhall Station, I felt as if I were going among friends, for they were very good to me at Millbank. "Habron, don't you know me?" the chief warder asked, "I am very glad to see you back".'[72]

The communication problems between authorities and staff continued when, as the chief warder went off somewhere for a few minutes, the prison warders set about putting William to work picking oakum with some other prisoners.[73] This order was belayed as soon as the chief returned and William was then brought to a door that was opened to reveal Mr Deakin standing alongside the prison governor. For the first time William realised that he was being released. He was heard to comment that 'he was sure the day of his release would come'.[74]

As he pondered on what had happened to him, he said that the verdict of guilty followed by the death sentence had been a shock that he could barely take in at the time. 'I never believed that I could ever be brought in guilty,' he said, 'and when I was condemned I felt sure I could not be hanged.' It was his religious faith and the support of his priest that had kept him going thought the dark times. '... if it had not been for the priest I do not know how I should have lived on at all,' he said. 'As it was, I prayed day and night, and never quite lost hope.'

Through all the bad times, it seems, he fought to keep his hope in the justice system alive too. He told himself repeatedly, 'I know that I am innocent of the crime, and an innocent man will never be allowed to suffer for the guilty.'[75]

The process of his execution had advanced as far as the hangman taking a professional look at him. 'Marwood had actually been to look at me to measure my size and weight,' William said. 'Luckily I did not know who the man was who looked at me so curiously till afterwards.'[76] When asked about the police role in his conviction he said, 'They betrayed me with the footprint. It was a police affair altogether. A policeman had been killed; and they meant to hang somebody for it.'[77] That was all he said about the police. According to one report at least, William chose not to indulge in personal attacks against those responsible for his conviction, '... he refrains from making specific charges against individuals, or attacking particular portions of the evidence against him'.[78]

He did speak to newspaper reporters about his time in prison and how hard it had been for him:

Three pounds of oakum is a heavy job, sir, I can tell you, and is mighty severe on the hands; but it is nothing to the work in the West Quarry at Portland, where I have been for a long time past … as I was young and a labourer I was kept hard at the outdoor work.[79]

He also had a strong sense of having lost precious time:

Just think, sir, that I was arrested on the 1st of August, 1876, and have never breathed the free air, nor known the taste of tobacco, since then till this moment. And all lost … Nothing makes me so sorry as thinking of my lost time.[80]

He regretted that the time could not have been spent learning a new skill that would have been of use to him now on his release:

… what is worst of all, I have learnt nothing in prison in all this long time … Some lucky prisoners are allowed to learn a trade, and I begged to be allowed to learn tailoring or shoemaking, that I might have a trade when I came out … Here I come out of prison just as ignorant and helpless as when I went in, while other men, not supposed to be so strong as I am, have learnt how to get their bread without lifting and dragging …[81]

William and Mr Deakin were brought to St Pancras Station where they boarded the five o'clock Midland train for Manchester. They could be seen sitting in the carriage, chatting and smoking cigars, as they waited for the their train to pull out of the station.

As they travelled towards Manchester it soon became clear that the government's plans for a low-profile release were foiled. News of William's freedom spread rapidly and cheering crowds gathered to support him at stations all along the route. A man in Bedford even presented him with £5 and another in Leicester gave him half a sovereign.[82]

Arriving in Manchester around ten o'clock an emotional reunion took place between William Habron and his two brothers, John and Frank. William's joy was not to last long, however, as his brothers had some very bad news to impart; during his stay in prison his father had died back home in Ireland. The family had decided not to burden William with the sad news while he was still suffering in prison. The old man had reportedly been 'broken hearted' about what had happened to his son.[83] Understandably, William did not take the news well. 'Habron was much affected by the news, as he said he had relied upon the hope of sooner or later being able to prove to this father and mother his innocence of the crime for which he has suffered.'[84]

Within days William Habron and his brother John left for Ireland. His arrival home was celebrated by the local populace in Mayo and Roscommon, who had followed the developments in this tragic story from the beginning:

Habron arrived on Friday evening from Dublin at Ballyhaunis, County Mayo. The population turned out, headed by their brass band, and accompanied Habron a mile through the town, on the road to his native village, Cloonfad. Bonfires were lighted at night.[85]

When it came to light that although Mr Habron had been declared an innocent man he was transported to London in handcuffs, the Home Secretary was forced to admit the fact in the House of Commons and accept responsibility for it:

I had thought, from the intimation I sent to Portland, that, although they were not aware that he was to be actually released, they would not have treated him in the way they did; but I am bound to say, in justice to [the] officials, that if it had struck me for a moment that they would do so, I certainly would have given more positive directions. I can only regret what has taken place, and for the absence of those positive instructions which I ought to have given I take the entire blame on myself.[86]

As for Katherine Dyson, the other person whose life had been greatly affected by the criminal actions of Charles Peace, she too was seeking freedom of a kind. The Banner Cross murder case had given her both fame and infamy. Wherever she went, she was followed by crowds of people and had to be given police protection. She decided that the best option for her was a return to America. She departed Sheffield for Liverpool on her way to the United States on 19 February 1879.[87] As she boarded the ship she gave a statement to the assembled press from which it was clear that her resentment towards Peace had not abated following his sentencing:

My opinion is that Peace is a perfect demon – not a man. The place to which the wicked go is not bad enough for him. I think its occupants, bad as they might be, are too good to be where he is … My lifelong regret will be that I ever knew him.[88]

The **End** of a **Life** of **Villainy**

Reverend Littlewood acknowledged Peace's confession to the murder of Constable Cock as 'an act of justice' but he wanted Peace to go further.[89] He now wanted him to reveal the names of those who had received stolen goods from him over the years. He tried to persuade Peace about the spiritual benefits of such a confession:

> I have no hesitation in saying that such a disclosure would be greatly to your benefit in the sight of God ... You committed a great injustice to society, and now I ask you to do an act of justice to society, and I ask you to do it as well for your own sake.[90]

Peace was not receptive to the idea. In any case, he always downplayed the importance of those to whom he had sold the stolen goods:

> You know, Sir, the public generally look on this kind of thing in the same light as you do. It is quite a mistake. I suppose you mean to say, Sir, that if there were no receivers there would be no stealers ... I assure you, Sir, that the impression is wrong.[91]

He explained to the clergyman how, for the most part, he had worked alone, even to the extent of removing all the precious stones from the stolen jewellery himself and melting down the gold and silver.[92]

Peace was not prepared to make any more confessions, but he did want Reverend Littlewood to do something for him. He requested that the clergyman preach a special sermon after his execution all about his life. 'I want all who have known me,' he said, 'to have me stated exactly as I am, that in the end my death may not be altogether without service to society.'[93] He was adamant that the people of Darnall could have nothing bad to say against him. Conveniently forgetting about the Dysons and those many victims that he had robbed over the years, he said, 'I never did any of them any harm all the time I was there'.[94] Apart from perpetuating his legacy, the other reason he wanted the sermon preached was for the good of his family members. He was worried that they might suffer for his actions after his death. He had advised them on how to deal with such a situation should it arise. His advice does not accord with how one imagines he would have dealt with such an event himself, 'If any people are so mean as to sneer at you because of me, put it down to their badness and take my advice and leave it to their foolishness and God to deal with them'.[95]

He believed, rather naively, that a carefully worded sermon from Reverend Littlewood would help:

> I hope you will preach my funeral sermon of advice to the people of Darnall on Sunday next, and tell them that my life has been a very bad, wicked, and base one, full of misery and imprisonment. I hope and trust they will take warning by my most miserable life and end. I hope and trust that they will have mercy and compassion upon every member of my family, and not insult them or cast slurs or remarks at them upon my account, for they cannot help anything that I have done.[96]

As the date of his execution approached, Peace seemed to be adopting a rather equanimous attitude to his predicament. He wrote to his family saying that he would not have wanted to serve out his sentence for the attack on Constable Robinson and would, most likely, have died in prison anyway:

> You must understand that I should have had a long and dreary and miserable life of imprisonment, for imprisonment is much harder now than it has ever been known, and if I had nothing against my character I should have had to have been twenty years before I could be recommended for my freedom, and even then it would entirely depend upon the merits of the case. So that I think I should never have gained my freedom, but should have died a miserable death on a prison bed, surrounded by a class of men anything but good and God-fearing.[97]

Of course, this may have been no more than an attempt on his part to make his death easier for his family to accept.

On 24 February, the day before his execution, Peace suddenly heard the sound of loud hammering coming from somewhere in the prison. He knew immediately what it was. 'That's a noise that would make some men fall on the floor,' he said to his gaolers. 'They are working at my scaffold.' The warders tried to comfort him by lying and telling him that he was wrong. Peace was too wily to be fooled so easily and he knew that he was listening to the sound of someone working with the type of timber known as deal. 'I have not worked so long with wood,' he said, 'without knowing the sound of deals; and they don't have deals inside a prison for anything else than scaffolds.'[98]

He spent some time that day in his prison cell with his wife Hannah, his stepson Willie, his daughter Jane Bolsover and her husband. The Bolsovers also brought their recently born first child, his grandchild, for him to see.[99] It was the last of a

Charles Peace had grown remarkably aged in appearance as he approached the end. (Topfoto)

number of visits that he had received from his family members. Only a few weeks earlier he had drawn up his will in which he bequeathed all his possessions to his wife Hannah.[100]

During their final visit he asked his relatives to restrain themselves from showing too much emotion as, he said, he did not want to be affected by it. He gave instructions that after his execution they should sell or exhibit all his works of art, including the design that he had drawn for a monument over his grave. He gave his wife a prototype of a funeral card that he had designed:

In Memory of Charles Peace
Who was executed in Armley Prison
Tuesday February 25th 1879
Aged 47

For that I don but never intended

After some time, he asked whether they had anything else that they wanted to say to him and Hannah reminded him that he had promised to pray with them before they left. This he did on his knees for about half an hour. The newspapers reported that he included prayers for the Habron brothers and the relatives of the two men that he had killed.[101] As his relatives departed he shook each of them by the hand in turn, blessed them and began to cry.

The night before his execution, Peace received a visit from Mr Keene, the prison governor. The chaplain, Reverend Osmond Cookson, stayed with him until three o'clock in the morning and then Peace managed to sleep until a quarter to six.[102]

The morning of 25 February 1879 began bitterly cold with a sharp frost on the ground.[103] Peace began the day, perhaps surprisingly for a man about to die, by consuming a substantial breakfast of toast, bacon, eggs and tea.[104] He even expressed his dissatisfaction about the quality of the bacon supplied by the prison.

Shortly before he was due to be taken to the gallows, Peace wrote some final letters to his family. To Hannah he wrote:

I tell you this great joy that I could not tell you yesterday – for I could not. No fear now, for it is all cleared up as to where I am going to. I am going to Heaven, or to the place that the good go to who die in the Lord, to the place appointed by my God for the good to wait until the resurrection of the dead. So do not forget our meeting place is in Heaven. So do come at the last, and you will find me there. This letter is wrote twenty-five minutes before I go to die so I must now say 'Good-bye' to all. So good-bye – good-bye, and God bless you all, for I am going to Heaven. – Charles Peace.[105]

To his brother:

> I write to you, hoping you will take this as a warning from the scaffold, as I intend it to be handed to my chaplain when upon the scaffold the moment before I die.
>
> I am sorry to say that I have been a very bad, base, and wicked man the whole course of my life. None but God and myself know the extent of my terrible deeds. And what has it all profited me now?
>
> Oh, let me beg of you in my last moments to give yourself to God and try and walk in the narrow path that leads to eternal life. And may the great God in His merciful goodness pardon all your sins, and may we all meet in the end at His right hand in glory.
>
> I have prayed to the great and all-powerful God to forgive me all my sins, as I freely forgive all who may have sinned against me.
>
> That these few lines may have the desired effect upon you is the dying prayer of – Your Brother.[106]

At one point, the door to Peace's cell opened and a grey haired gentleman in his sixties walked in, flanked by a number of prison officials. It was Mr William Marwood, the famous hangman and shoemaker from Horncastle in Lincolnshire. Marwood was reputed with being the first to introduce the so-called 'long drop' method of hanging, before which prisoners used to struggle and wriggle until death was usually caused by strangulation. With Marwood's modern method the condemned prisoner fell a distance of 6–10ft and died instantly for the most part, and apparently painlessly, of a broken neck. Apart from the lessened suffering of the prisoner, the modern method was easier for those present at the execution to observe.

Marwood was the official hangman for London and Middlesex, for which he was paid £20 per year and £10 for each execution. He also travelled the rest of the country plying his gruesome trade while, of course, not neglecting his cobbling business in Horncastle. Marwood was very proud of his position as executioner, even having business cards on which were printed his name, address and simply the word 'executioner'.

There is a story that Peace had once met Mr Marwood while in disguise and on the run after the Banner Cross murder. The story goes that Peace was on a train and began to chat with a man in the carriage who eventually told him that he was the well-known executioner. As Marwood was getting off the train, Peace is reputed to have said to him, 'If ever you have to do the job for me, be sure you grease the rope well to let me slip'.[107] Marwood, the story goes, laughed at the joke, little realising the irony of the situation.

It is not known if any such encounter was discussed by the two men on the morning of Peace's execution, but Marwood did visit the condemned man at the governor's request. Peace wanted to clarify something with him. 'I am glad to see you, Mr Marwood,' he said, 'I wish to have a word with you. I do hope you will not punish me. I hope you will do your work quickly.'[108] Marwood assured him that he would and Peace seemed satisfied. Peace could be sure that this execution would be performed just as professionally as all of Marwood's other assignments.

At eight o'clock, as the prison bell tolled, Peace was led from the prison building to the gallows in procession behind the governor, the undersheriff and the chaplain who read out loud from scripture as he walked. Peace was flanked by prison warders. His appearance was described in *The Times* the following day: 'He walked with a firm and buoyant tread, and showed no signs of either excitement or fear. His face, though, had a wan and haggard look, but his health appeared to be in a much better state than it was on the day of his trial.'[109]

Another newspaper correspondent gave his impressions of the scene:

> … there was nothing in his gait to indicate that he would not be able to fulfil his oft-expressed desire that he should be able to undergo his sentence with fortitude … It was noticed that instead of walking with downcast eyes, as is often the case in such circumstances, Peace looked about him as if to distinguish who were standing near.[110]

As soon as Peace had mounted those six steps leading to the gallows, Marwood began to bind his legs. He then placed the noose around the prisoner's neck. Peace remained calm throughout. But as the chaplain was reciting prayers and Marwood went to put the white cap over Peace's head, he snapped, 'Don't; I want to look'.[111] Marwood stopped.

Peace then joined in the prayers, 'God have mercy upon me, Lord have mercy upon me, Christ have mercy upon me'. Thinking that he was now ready, Marwood once again tried to place the white cap over his head, but Peace stopped him, saying, 'Don't; stop a bit, if you please'.[112] Ever the man for the performance, Peace then turned to the four members of the press who were in attendance and addressed his final comments to them:

> You gentleman reporters, I wish you to notice the few words I am going to say to you. I know that my life has been base and bad. I wish you to ask the world after you have seen my death what man could die as I die if he did not die in the fear of the Lord? Tell all my friends that I feel sure they have sincerely forgiven me, and that I am going into the Kingdom of Heaven, or else to that place prepared for us to rest in until the great Judgement Day. I have no enemies that I feel anything against on this earth. I wish all my enemies, or those would-be enemies – I wish them well, and I wish them to come to the Kingdom of Heaven at last. And now

to one and all I say good-bye, good-bye, Heaven bless you, and may you all come to the Kingdom of Heaven at last. Amen.[113]

He addressed some final comments to the welfare of his family:

> … my last wishes and my last respects are to my dear children and to their dear mother. I hope no person will disgrace them by taunting them or jeering at them on my account, but will have mercy upon them. God bless you, my children! My children, each good-bye. Heaven bless you! Good-bye. Amen. Oh, my Lord God, have mercy upon me![114]

After Marwood had finally placed the white cap over his head Peace asked for a cup of water, but was denied. The chaplain continued to pray and as he uttered the words, 'Lord Jesus receive his spirit', Marwood pulled the bolt and Charles Peace fell to his death, with what one writer described as 'an awful thud'.[115] The hangman had allowed a drop of 9ft 4in and the surgeon pronounced Peace's death to have been 'as nearly as possible instantaneous'.[116] He was 47 years of age.[117]

The body of Victorian Britain's infamous villain was buried in the grounds of Armley Gaol.

The truth is that Peace may well have committed many other murders, apart from those of Cock and Dyson. Whenever anyone had tried to apprehend him in the course of a burglary he was very quick to produce a firearm and, if necessary, use it with fatal consequences. At least one former inspector of prisons, who knew him well, thought so. 'There is strong reason to believe,' he said, 'that he committed many more murders than ever came to light …'[118]

Yet, even before his death, Peace's place in popular history was being marked by the addition of a wax tableau of him in Madame Tussaud's Chamber of Horrors. For 6d from 10.00 a.m. to 10.00 p.m. curious visitors could attend and look upon the form of Charles Peace, once Victorian Britain's most wanted man.[119]

Notes

Part One

Chapter 1

1 Shore (ed.), *Trials of Charles Frederick Peace*, p.14, the evidence of Simpson.
2 *The Times*, 29 November 1876.
3 *Ibid.*
4 *Ibid.*; Shore (ed.), *Trials of Charles Frederick Peace*, p.15, the evidence of Constable Beanland.
5 *Ibid.*
6 *The Times*, 29 November 1876; Shore (ed.), *Trials of Charles Frederick Peace*, pp.15, 16, the evidence of Constable Ewen.
7 Shore (ed.), *Trials of Charles Frederick Peace*, p.17, the evidence of Sergeant Thompson.
8 *The Times*, 29 November 1876; Shore (ed.), *Trials of Charles Frederick Peace*, p.17, the evidence of Dr Dill.
9 His age given on the headstone on his grave; Shore (ed.), *Trials of Charles Frederick Peace*, p.11.
10 *The Times*, 29 November 1876.
11 Shore (ed.), *Trials of Charles Frederick Peace*, p.15, the evidence of Dr Dill.
12 *The Times*, 29 November 1876, for the statement that he had suspected these three men 'at once'.

Chapter 2

13 Bent, J., *Criminal Life: Reminiscences of Forty-Two Years as a Police Officer*, p.180; Durston, G. J., *Burglars and Bobbies: Crime and Policing in Victorian London*, p.230.
14 Crofton, H. T., *A History of the Ancient Chapel of Stretford in Manchester Parish including Sketches of the Township of Stretford together with Notices of Local Families and Persons*, printed for the Chetham Society, 1903.
15 *Manchester Evening News*, 29 January 2010, plaque erected in his honour for this charitable work.
16 Crofton, H. T., *A History of the Ancient Chapel of Stretford in Manchester Parish including Sketches of the Township of Stretford together with Notices of Local Families and Persons*, printed for the Chetham Society, 1903.

17   Although the correct spelling of the surname is almost certainly 'Hebron', as
      nearly all the records and newspaper reports from the time use the spelling
      'Habron' I have decided, for convenience, to use that version here. Records show,
      however, that there were no families named Habron living in their home place
      of Cloonfad around that time, while there *was* a family called Hebron (see census
      records, Ireland). In the letter sent from John to Mr Megson in 1877, he spells his
      own name as 'John Hebron' (see Shore (ed.), *Trials of Charles Frederick Peace*, p.41).

18   *The Times*, 12 March 1879. This story is told by a letter writer to the newspaper
      who signed himself as 'D', dated 10 March 1879.

19   Shore (ed.), *Trials of Charles Frederick Peace*, p.12.

20   Bent, J., *Criminal Life: Reminiscences of Forty-Two Years as a Police Officer*, p.236.

21   *Ibid.* p.236.

22   *Ibid.* p.236.

23   Shore (ed.), *Trials of Charles Frederick Peace*, p.22, the evidence of Deakin.

24   Bent, J., *Criminal Life: Reminiscences of Forty-Two Years as a Police Officer*, p.237.

25   *Ibid.* p.238.

26   *Ibid.* p.238.

27   Ward, D., *The King of the Lags*, p.87.

28   Bent, J., *Criminal Life: Reminiscences of Forty-Two Years as a Police Officer*, p.238;
      Shore (ed.), *Trials of Charles Frederick Peace*, p.18, the evidence of Superintendent
      Bent.

29   Shore (ed.), *Trials of Charles Frederick Peace*, p.17.

30   *Ibid.* p.12.

31   'Slutch' is a local word for mud; Shore (ed.), *Trials of Charles Frederick Peace*, p.12.

32   Shore (ed.), *Trials of Charles Frederick Peace*, p.22.

33   *Ibid.* p.18.

34   Bent, J., *Criminal Life: Reminiscences of Forty-Two Years as a Police Officer*, p.239.

35   Shore (ed.), *Trials of Charles Frederick Peace*, pp.19, 20.

36   *Ibid.* p.18.

37   *Ibid.* p.18.

38   Bent, J., *Criminal Life: Reminiscences of Forty-Two Years as a Police Officer*, p.241.

39   Shore (ed.), *Trials of Charles Frederick Peace*, p.19.

40   *Ibid.* p.21.

41   *Ibid.* p.23.

42   Letter published in *The Times*, 12 March 1879.

43   *Ibid.*

44   *Ibid.*

45   Supplement to the *Evening Post*, Wellington, New Zealand, 17 May 1879.

46   *The Times*, 12 May 1879.

Chapter 3

47   Shore (ed.), *Trials of Charles Frederick Peace*, pp.10, 11.

48   *Ibid.*, p.12; the *Times*, 29 November 1876.

49   *The Times*, 29 November 1876.

50   Shore (ed.), *Trials of Charles Frederick Peace*, p.13; *The Times*, 29 November 1876.

51   Shore (ed.), *Trials of Charles Frederick Peace*, p.13; *The Times*, 29 November 1876.

52   Shore (ed.), *Trials of Charles Frederick Peace*, p.13.

53   *Ibid.* p.13.
54   *Ibid.* p.14.
55   *Ibid.* p.15.
56   *Ibid.* p.15.
57   *Ibid.* p.15.
58   *The Times*, 29 November 1876.
59   Shore (ed.), *Trials of Charles Frederick Peace*, p.14.
60   *Ibid.* pp.16, 17.
61   *Ibid.* p.15.

Chapter 4

62   Shore (ed.), *Trials of Charles Frederick Peace*, p.18, 19, the evidence of
     Superintendent Bent; *The Times*, 29 November 1876.
63   Shore (ed.), *Trials of Charles Frederick Peace*, p.20.
64   *Ibid.* pp.18, 19. Transcript of the trial of the Habrons, and the evidence of Love.
65   *Ibid.* p.22, the evidence of Deakin; *The Times*, 29 November 1876.
66   Shore (ed.), *Trials of Charles Frederick Peace*, p.22, the evidence of Deakin; the
     Times, 29 November 1876.
67   Shore (ed.), *Trials of Charles Frederick Peace*, p.22.
68   *Ibid.* p.22.
69   Bent, J., *Criminal Life: Reminiscences of Forty-Two Years as a Police Officer*, p.242.
70   *Ibid.* p.21.
71   *Ibid.* p.21.
72   *Ibid.* p.21.
73   *Ibid.* p.22.
74   *Ibid.* p.23.
75   *Ibid.* p.24.
76   Bent, J., *Criminal Life: Reminiscences of Forty-Two Years as a Police Officer*, p.241.
77   Shore (ed.), *Trials of Charles Frederick Peace*, p.24.

Chapter 5

78   Shore (ed.), *Trials of Charles Frederick Peace*, p.25.
79   *Ibid.* p.26.
80   *Ibid.* p.26, quoted from Inspector Henderson's notebook.
81   *Ibid.* p.27.
82   *Ibid.* p.27.
83   *Ibid.* p.27.
84   *Ibid.* p.28.

Chapter 6

85   Shore (ed.), *Trials of Charles Frederick Peace*, p.28, transcript of the trial of the
     Habrons, Leresche's speech for the defence.
86   *Ibid.* p.29.
87   *Ibid.* pp.28, 29.
88   *Ibid.* p.29.

 89 *Ibid.* p.29.
 90 *Ibid.* p.29.
 91 *Ibid.* p.29.
 92 *Ibid.* p.29.
 93 *Ibid.* p.29.
 94 *Ibid.* p.31.
 95 *Ibid.* p.29.
 96 *Ibid.* p.31.
 97 *Ibid.* p.31.
 98 *Ibid.* p.30.
 99 *Ibid.* p.31.
100 *Ibid.* p.31.
101 *Ibid.* p.32.
102 *Ibid.* p.32.
103 *Ibid.* p.32.
104 *Ibid.* p.32.
105 *Ibid.* p.32.
106 *Ibid.* p.33.
107 *Ibid.* p.33.

Chapter 7

108 Shore (ed.), *Trials of Charles Frederick Peace*, p.33.
109 *Ibid.* p.33.
110 *Ibid.* p.33.
111 *Ibid.* p.33.
112 *Ibid.* p.33.
113 *Ibid.* p.34.
114 *Ibid.* p.34.
115 *Ibid.* p.34.
116 *Ibid.* p.34.
117 *Ibid.* pp.34, 35.
118 *Ibid.* p.34.
119 *Ibid.* p.35.
120 *Ibid.* p.34.
121 *Ibid.* p.35.
122 *Ibid.* pp.35, 36.
123 *Ibid.* p.36.
124 *Ibid.* pp.35, 36.
125 *Ibid.* p.36.
126 *Ibid.* p.36.
127 *Ibid.* pp.36, 37.
128 *Ibid.* p.37
129 *Ibid.* p.37.
130 *Ibid.* p.37.
131 *Ibid.* p.37.
132 Ward, D., *The King of the Lags*, p.95.
133 Bent, J., *Criminal Life: Reminiscences of Forty-Two Years as a Police Officer*, p.242.

Part Two

Chapter 8

1   Ward, *The King of the Lags*, p.65.
2   Shore (ed.), *Trials of Charles Frederick Peace*, p.177.
3   *Ibid.* p.48.
4   Shore (ed.), *Trials of Charles Frederick Peace*, p.74, the hearing at Sheffield before the stipendiary magistrate, the evidence of Mary Ann Gregory; Shore (ed.), *Trials of Charles Frederick Peace*, p.186, the inquest into death of Arthur Dyson, the evidence of Mary Ann Gregory.
5   *Ibid.* p.186.
6   *Ibid.* p.186.
7   Shore (ed.), *Trials of Charles Frederick Peace*, p.74, the hearing at Sheffield before the stipendiary magistrate, the evidence of Sarah Colgreaves; Shore (ed.), *Trials of Charles Frederick Peace*, p.144, Banner Cross murder trial before Mr Justice Lopes, the evidence of Sarah Colgreaves.
8   *Ibid.* p.74.
9   *Ibid.* p.77.
10 *Ibid.* p.77.
11 *Ibid.* p.188.
12 *Ibid.* p.77.
13 *Ibid.* p.72.
14 Peace's own account in *The Times*, 26 February 1879; Shore (ed.), *Trials of Charles Frederick Peace*, p.70, the hearing at Sheffield before the stipendiary magistrate, the evidence of Katherine Dyson.
15 Shore (ed.), *Trials of Charles Frederick Peace*, p.81, the hearing at Sheffield before the stipendiary magistrate, the evidence of Dr Harrison.
16 *Ibid.* p.81; *The Times*, 18 January 1879.

Chapter 9

17 Ward, D., *The King of the Lags*, p.30 for smallpox.
18 Anon., *The Master Criminal. The Life Story of Charles Peace*, pp.96, 97.
19 Postgate, R.W., *Murder, Piracy and Treason: a selection of notable English Trials*, p.221; Walbrook, H. M., *Murders and Murder Trials, 1812–1912*, p.200.
20 *Ibid.*
21 Whibley, C., 'Two Cracksmen', in *The New Review*, October 1895, p.427.
22 Shore (ed.), *Trials of Charles Frederick Peace*, p.5, quoting from *Manchester Evening Mail*, 25 February 1879; Ward, D., *The King of the Lags*, p.46.

Chapter 10

23 Shore (ed.), *Trials of Charles Frederick Peace*, p.40, quote from Sir Archibald Bodkin.
24 Told in Anon., *The Master Criminal. The Life Story of Charles Peace*, pp.89–92.
25 *Ibid.* p.91.

Chapter 11

26　Ward, D., *The King of the Lags*, p.67, quoting from the *Sheffield Independent*.

27　Shore (ed.), *Trials of Charles Frederick Peace*, p.48.

28　*Ibid*. p.48.

29　*Ibid*. p.48.

30　*Sheffield Independent*, 30 November 1876.

31　Shore (ed.), *Trials of Charles Frederick Peace*, p.49.

32　Irving, H. B., *A Book of Remarkable Criminals*, p.38.

33　Shore (ed.), *Trials of Charles Frederick Peace*, p.49.

34　*Ibid*. p.50.

35　*Ibid*. p.49.

36　*Ibid*. p.49.

37　*Ibid*. pp.49, 50.

38　*Ibid*. p.49.

39　*Ibid*. pp.49, 50.

40　*Ibid*. p.50.

41　*Ibid*. p.149, the Banner Cross murder trial before Mr Justice Lopes, the evidence of Rose Annie Sykes.

42　*Ibid*. p.69.

43　*Ibid*. p.187.

Chapter 12

44　*The Times*, 26 February 1879.

45　*Ibid*.

46　*The Times*, 25 January 1879; Shore (ed.), *Trials of Charles Frederick Peace*, p.69.

47　Shore (ed.), *Trials of Charles Frederick Peace*, p.74, the inquest into the death of Arthur Dyson, the evidence of Mary Ann Gregory.

48　*Ibid*. p.70.

49　*The Times*, 2 December 1876.

50　Shore (ed.), *Trials of Charles Frederick Peace*, the notes are printed on pp.173–76. Where I have quoted directly from the notes, in the interest of simplicity and clarity and where it does not alter the meaning, I have made some minor changes to spelling, capitalisation and punctuation.

51　This point is made, for example, in Shore (ed.), *Trials of Charles Frederick Peace*, at the end of p.175.

52　Shore (ed.), *Trials of Charles Frederick Peace*, p.184, the inquest into the death of Arthur Dyson, the statement made by the coroner.

53　*The Times*, 9 December 1876.

54　Shore (ed.), *Trials of Charles Frederick Peace*, p.186.

55　*Ibid*. p.186.

56　*Ibid*. p.187.

57　*Ibid*. p.190.

58　*Ibid*. pp.190, 191.

Chapter 13

59   This version issued in December of 1876; Shore (ed.), *Trials of Charles Frederick Peace*, p.52; Anon., *The Master Criminal*, p.43.

60   Berrey, R. J. Power, *The Bye-Ways of Crime with Some Stories from the Black Museum*, p.8.

61   *The Times*, 25 January 1879.

62   Anon., *The Master Criminal. The Life Story of Charles Peace*, p.98.

63   *Ibid.* p.96.

64   Shore (ed.), *Trials of Charles Frederick Peace*, p.43; Anon., *The Master Criminal*, p.124.

65   *The Times*, 25 January 1879.

66   *Ibid.*

67   Shore (ed.), *Trials of Charles Frederick Peace*, p.50.

Chapter 14

68   Shore (ed.), *Trials of Charles Frederick Peace*, p.53.

69   *The Times*, 26 February 1879.

70   *Ibid.*

71   *The Times*, 25 January 1879; *The Times*, 26 February 1879; Irving, H. B., *A Book of Remarkable Criminals*, p. 49; Ward, D., *The King of the Lags*, p.122.

72   *The Times*, 1 February 1879.

73   Ward, D., *The King of the Lags*, p.59.

74   Told in Anon., *The Master Criminal. The Life Story of Charles Peace*, pp.68–72.

75   *Ibid.* p.72.

76   Ward, D., *The King of the Lags*, p.123.

77   Anon., *The Master Criminal. The Life Story of Charles Peace*, p.51.

78   *The Times*, 1 January 1877.

79   *Ibid.*

80   *Ibid.* 4 January 1877.

Chapter 15

81   *The Times*, 26 February 1879.

82   Anon., *The Master Criminal. The Life Story of Charles Peace*, p.65.

83   *The Times*, 26 February 1879.

84   Shore (ed.), *Trials of Charles Frederick Peace*, p.54.

85   Estimated values from 'Crimes and Criminals' in *Strand Magazine: An illustrated Monthly*, January 1894, p.284.

86   Irving, H. B., *A Book of Remarkable Criminals*, p. 52; Anon., *The Master Criminal. The Life Story of Charles Peace*, p.66.

87   *The Times*, 11 February 1879.

88   *Ibid.*

89   *Ibid.*

90   Anon., *The Master Criminal. The Life Story of Charles Peace*, p.121.

91   Berrey, R. J. Power, *The Bye-Ways of Crime with Some Stories from the Black Museum*, pp.66, 67.

92   'Crimes and Criminals' in *Strand Magazine: An illustrated Monthly*, January 1894, p.284.
93   For information on his tools see Griffiths, *Mysteries of Police and Crime*, Vol. 2 (1899), p.183; Berrey, R. J. Power, *The Bye-Ways of Crime with Some Stories from the Black Museum*, pp.8–10; *The Times*, 1 February 1879.
94   Anon., *The Master Criminal. The Life Story of Charles Peace*, p.76.
95   *The Times*, 5 February 1879; there is also mention of how he worked alone in Griffiths, *Mysteries of Police and Crime*, Vol. 1 (1899), p.320.
96   *The Times*, 27 February 1879.
97   *The Times*, 18 November 1878.
98   *The Times*, 25 January 1879.
99   *Ibid*.

Part Three

Chapter 16

1   *The Times*, 8 November 1878.
2   Shore (ed.), *Trials of Charles Frederick Peace*, pp.55, 57, the trial of John Ward, alias Charles Peace, at the Old Bailey before Mr Justice Hawkins, the evidence of Constable Robinson.
3   *Ibid*. p.57.
4   *London Daily Chronicle*, 11 October 1878.
5   Old Bailey Proceedings Online, November 1878, the trial of John Ward alias Charles Peace (t18781118-51), the evidence of Constable Body.

Chapter 17

6   *The Times*, 26 October 1878.
7   Old Bailey Proceedings Online, January 1879, the trial of Hannah Peace alias Ward (t18790113-193), evidence of Brion (spelt Bryan here); Ward, D., *The King of the Lags*, p.22; Irving, H. B., *A Book of Remarkable Criminals*, 'The Life of Charles Peace', p.58.
8   *The Times*, 19 December 1878.
9   Old Bailey Proceedings Online, January 1879, the trial of Hannah Peace alias Ward (t18790113-193), evidence of Inspector Phillips.
10   *The Times*, 7 November 1878.
11   The *Daily Telegraph*, 13 November 1878.
12   *Ibid*.
13   *The Times*, 8 November 1878.
14   *The Times*, 8 February 1879.
15   *Ibid*.
16   *Ibid*. 10 February 1879.

Chapter 18

17   Shore (ed.), *Trials of Charles Frederick Peace*, p.56; *The Times*, 20 November 1878.

18   Old Bailey Proceedings Online, November 1878, the trial of John Ward alias Charles Peace (t18781118-51), evidence of Constable Body; Shore (ed.), *Trials of Charles Frederick Peace*, pp.57, 59.

19   *The Times*, 20 November 1878.

20   *Ibid.*

21   *Ibid.*

22   Shore (ed.), *Trials of Charles Frederick Peace*, p.59, quoting Montagu Williams.

23   *Ibid.*

24   Anon., *The Master Criminal. The Life Story of Charles Peace*, p.107; Shore (ed.), *Trials of Charles Frederick Peace*, p.59, quoting Montagu Williams; Williams, M. S., *Leaves of a Life: Being the Reminiscences of Montagu Williams, Q.C.,* Vol. 2, pp.124–26.

25   Anon., *The Master Criminal. The Life Story of Charles Peace*, p.107; Shore (ed.), *Trials of Charles Frederick Peace*, p.60, quoting Montagu Williams; Williams, M. S., *Leaves of a Life: Being the Reminiscences of Montagu Williams, Q.C.,* Vol. 2, pp.124–26.

26   Shore (ed.), *Trials of Charles Frederick Peace*, p.60; Williams, M. S., *Leaves of a Life: Being the Reminiscences of Montagu Williams, Q.C.,* Vol. 2, pp.124–26.

27   Shore (ed.), *Trials of Charles Frederick Peace*, p.60; Williams, M. S., *Leaves of a Life: Being the Reminiscences of Montagu Williams, Q.C.,* Vol. 2, p.126.

28   Shore (ed.), *Trials of Charles Frederick Peace*, p.61.

29   *Ibid.* p.61

30   Old Bailey Proceedings Online, November 1878, the trial of John Ward alias Charles Peace (t18781118-51).

31   *The Times*, 20 November 1878.

32   *The Times*, 23 November 1878.

Chapter 19

33   *The Times*, 19 December 1878.

34   *Ibid.*

35   *Ibid.*

36   *The Times*, 19 September 1878.

37   *Ibid.*

38   *Ibid.*

39   *Ibid.*

40   *The Times*, 19 December 1878.

41   *Ibid.*

42   *Ibid.*

43   *Ibid.*

44   Ward, D., *The King of the Lags*, p.142.

45   Shore (ed.), *Trials of Charles Frederick Peace*, pp.61, 62 and 192; *The Times*, 15 January 1879.

46   Old Bailey Proceedings Online, January 1879, the trial of Hannah Peace alias Ward, (t18790113-193), the evidence of Inspector Twybell; Lamb, F., *Forty Years in the Old Bailey*, p.228.

47   Old Bailey Proceedings Online, January 1879, the trial of Hannah Peace alias Ward (t18790113-193).
48   *Ibid.*
49   *Ibid.*

Chapter 20

50   *The Times*, 20 November 1878.
51   *The Times*, 27 December 1878.
52   *The Times*, 8 January 1879; *Sheffield Daily Telegraph*, 7 January 1879.
53   Shore (ed.), *Trials of Charles Frederick Peace*, pp.62, 63.
54   *Ibid.*
55   *The Times*, 18 January 1879.
56   *Ibid.*
57   Shore (ed.), *Trials of Charles Frederick Peace*, pp.77, 65.
58   Unless otherwise stated, all direct speech from the hearing is adapted from Shore (ed.), *Trials of Charles Frederick Peace*, pp.64–108, the hearing at Sheffield before stipendiary magistrate.
59   *The Times*, 18 January 1879.
60   Shore (ed.), *Trials of Charles Frederick Peace*, pp.74, 77.
61   Shore (ed.), *Trials of Charles Frederick Peace*, p.76; *The Times*, 18 January 1879.
62   *The Times*, 18 January 1879.
63   *Ibid.*
64   *Ibid.*
65   Shore (ed.), *Trials of Charles Frederick Peace*, p.78; *The Times*, 18 January 1879.
66   Shore (ed.), *Trials of Charles Frederick Peace*, pp.82, 83.

Chapter 21

67   *The Times*, 23 January 1879.
68   *Ibid.*; Shore (ed.), *Trials of Charles Frederick Peace*, p.84.
69   *The Times*, 23 January 1879; Shore (ed.), *Trials of Charles Frederick Peace*, p.84.
70   *The Times*, 23 January 1879.
71   *The Times*, 24 January 1879.
72   Shore (ed.), *Trials of Charles Frederick Peace*, p.84; Anon., *The Master Criminal. The Life Story of Charles Peace*, p.107, for a slightly different version; Irving, H. B., *A Book of Remarkable Criminals*, p.64.
73   Shore (ed.), *Trials of Charles Frederick Peace*, pp.108, 109.
74   *The Times*, 24 January 1879.

Chapter 22

75   *The Times*, 25 January 1879.
76   *Ibid.*; Shore (ed.), *Trials of Charles Frederick Peace*, p.85.
77   Shore (ed.), *Trials of Charles Frederick Peace*, p.85.
78   *The Times*, 25 January 1879.
79   Shore (ed.), *Trials of Charles Frederick Peace*, p.86.
80   *The Times*, 25 January 1879; Shore (ed.), *Trials of Charles Frederick Peace*, p.86.

81 *The Times*, 25 January 1879.

82 Shore (ed.), *Trials of Charles Frederick Peace*, see note at the end of p.87.

83 *The Times*, 30 January 1879.

84 The following account of the cross-examination is adapted from the versions printed in *The Times*, 25 January 1879 and Shore (ed.), *Trials of Charles Frederick Peace*, pp.64–108.

85 Shore (ed.), *Trials of Charles Frederick Peace*, p.90, see note at the end of the page but, as stated in Ward, D., *The King of the Lags*, p.106, the chief constable of Sheffield made inquiries about Peace's claim and informed the Home Office that he had found evidence to prove that the Dysons were married.

Chapter 23

86 All courtroom dialogue in this chapter is adapted from the versions printed in *The Times*, 25 January 1879 and Shore (ed.), *Trials of Charles Frederick Peace*, pp.64–108.

Chapter 24

87 Clegg's brief for Peace's defence, Sheffield Archives, ref. 623/Z1/1-3; Ward, D., *The King of the Lags*, p.150.

88 *The Times*, 25 January 1879.

89 *The Times*, 27 January 1879.

90 *Ibid.*

91 *Ibid.*

92 *Ibid.*

93 *The Times*, 30 January 1879.

94 *Ibid.*

95 *Ibid.*

96 *Ibid.*

97 Shore (ed.), *Trials of Charles Frederick Peace*, pp.108, 109.

Chapter 25

98 *The Times*, 30 January 1879.

99 Deans, R. S., *Notable Trials: Romances of the Law Courts*, p.193.

100 *Ibid.* p.194.

101 Shore (ed.), *Trials of Charles Frederick Peace*, p.110.

102 *The Times*, 5 February 1879.

103 Shore (ed.), *Trials of Charles Frederick Peace*, p.112.

104 *Ibid.* pp.117, 118.

105 *The Times*, 2 February 1879.

106 *The Times*, 5 February 1879.

107 All of the following courtroom dialogue is adapted, unless otherwise stated, from the versions printed in *The Times*, 5 February 1879, and Shore (ed.), *Trials of Charles Frederick Peace*, pp.111–65.

108 *The Times*, 5 February 1879.

109 *Ibid.*

110 *Ibid.*

111 *Ibid.*
112 *Ibid.*

Chapter 26

113 *The Times*, 5 February 1879.
114 *Ibid.*
115 *Ibid.*
116 Shore (ed.), *Trials of Charles Frederick Peace*, p.147.
117 *The Times*, 5 February 1879.
118 *Ibid.*
119 *Ibid.*
120 Shore (ed.), *Trials of Charles Frederick Peace*, p.149.
121 Some of the newspapers later tried to cast doubt on his evidence by saying that
     he had been forced to admit, under cross-examination, that 'the rifle was of a
     common kind, such as was sent over to this country from Belgium in thousands'.
     Woodward objected strongly to the claim that this comment weakened his
     evidence in any way. He later clarified his view by stating that he was 'convinced'
     the bullets were fired from the same weapon. See *The Times*, 5 February 1879 and
     28 February 1879.

Chapter 27

122 *The Times*, 5 February 1879.
123 Shore (ed.), *Trials of Charles Frederick Peace*, p.152.
124 *Ibid.*
125 *Ibid.*
126 *Ibid.*
127 *Ibid.*
128 *Ibid.*
129 *Ibid.*
130 *Ibid.* p.153.
131 *Ibid.*
132 *Ibid.*; *The Times*, 5 February 1879.
133 Shore (ed.), *Trials of Charles Frederick Peace*, pp.153, 154.
134 Shore (ed.), *Trials of Charles Frederick Peace*, p.154.
135 *Ibid.*
136 *Ibid.*
137 *Ibid.*
138 *The Times*, 5 February 1879.
139 Shore (ed.), *Trials of Charles Frederick Peace*, p.154.
140 *The Times*, 5 February 1879.
141 Shore (ed.), *Trials of Charles Frederick Peace*, p.155.
142 *Ibid.*
143 *The Times*, 5 February 1879.
144 Shore (ed.), *Trials of Charles Frederick Peace*, p.157.
145 *Ibid.*

146 *The Times*, 5 February 1879; Shore (ed.), *Trials of Charles Frederick Peace*, pp.157, 158.

147 Shore (ed.), *Trials of Charles Frederick Peace*, p.160.

148 *The Times*, 5 February 1879.

149 Shore (ed.), *Trials of Charles Frederick Peace*, p.158.

150 *Ibid.*

151 *The Times*, 5 February 1879.

152 *The Times*, 5 February 1879; Shore (ed.), *Trials of Charles Frederick Peace*, p.160.

153 *The Times*, 5 February 1879; Shore (ed.), *Trials of Charles Frederick Peace*, p.161.

Chapter 28

154 *The Times*, 5 February 1879; Shore (ed.), *Trials of Charles Frederick Peace*, p.161.

155 Shore (ed.), *Trials of Charles Frederick Peace*, p.162.

156 *Ibid.*

157 *Ibid.*

158 *Ibid.*

159 *Ibid.* p.163.

160 *The Times*, 5 February 1879; Shore (ed.), *Trials of Charles Frederick Peace*, p.164.

161 *The Times*, 5 February 1879; Shore (ed.), *Trials of Charles Frederick Peace*, p.164.

162 Shore (ed.), *Trials of Charles Frederick Peace*, p.164; Anon., *The Master Criminal. The Life Story of Charles Peace*, p.118.

163 Shore (ed.), *Trials of Charles Frederick Peace*, pp.164, 165.

164 Anon., *The Master Criminal. The Life Story of Charles Peace*, p.118.

165 The *Spectator*, 8 February 1879, p.176.

Part Four

Chapter 29

1 *Daily Telegraph*, 8 February 1879.

2 Shore (ed.), *Trials of Charles Frederick Peace*, p.169.

3 *Ibid.*

4 Anon., *The Master Criminal. The Life Story of Charles Peace*, p.103.

5 Shore (ed.), *Trials of Charles Frederick Peace*, p.109 – the letter is dated 29 January 1879.

6 *Daily Telegraph*, 8 February 1879.

7 Anon., *The Master Criminal. The Life Story of Charles Peace*, p.123.

8 *Ibid.* p.121.

9 *Ibid.* pp.121, 122.

10 *The Times*, 26 February 1879.

11 Shore (ed.), *Trials of Charles Frederick Peace*, p.166.

12 *Ibid.*

13 *The Times*, 7 February 1879; *The Times*, 8 February 1879.

14 *The Times*, 7 February 1879.

15 *The Times*, 11 February 1879.

Chapter 30

16   *The Times*, 18 March 1879.

17   *The Times*, 20 December 1876.

18   Shore (ed.), *Trials of Charles Frederick Peace*, p.41.

19   *Ibid.* p.42.

20   *The Times*, 20 December 1876.

21   *The Times*, 28 February 1879.

22   Ward, D., *The King of the Lags*, p.88.

23   Supplement to the *Evening Post*, Wellington, New Zealand, 17 May 1879.

24   Shore (ed.), *Trials of Charles Frederick Peace*, p.43; *The Times*, 26 February 1879.

25   Shore (ed.), *Trials of Charles Frederick Peace*, p.43; *The Times*, 26 February 1879.

26   Shore (ed.), *Trials of Charles Frederick Peace*, p.45

27   *Ibid.*

28   Herbert, S., 'Criminal Confessions', in *The New Reader*, July 1896.

29   Anon., *The Master Criminal. The Life Story of Charles Peace*, pp.123, 124; Shore (ed.), *Trials of Charles Frederick Peace*, p.42; Ward, D., *The King of the Lags*, p.165.

30   Shore (ed.), *Trials of Charles Frederick Peace*, p.42.

31   *The Times*, 26 February 1879; Shore (ed.), *Trials of Charles Frederick Peace*, p.43.

32   *The Times*, 26 February 1879; Shore (ed.), *Trials of Charles Frederick Peace*, p.43.

33   *The Times*, 26 February 1879.

34   *Ibid.*; Shore (ed.), *Trials of Charles Frederick Peace*, p.44.

35   *The Times*, 26 February 1879; Shore (ed.), *Trials of Charles Frederick Peace*, p.44.

36   *The Times*, 26 February 1879; Shore (ed.), *Trials of Charles Frederick Peace*, p.42.

37   *The Times*, 3 March 1879.

38   Printed in Shore (ed.), *Trials of Charles Frederick Peace*, pp.44, 45.

39   *The Times*, 26 February 1879; Shore (ed.), *Trials of Charles Frederick Peace*, p.44.

40   Shore (ed.), *Trials of Charles Frederick Peace*, p.45 (spelling and grammar corrected here).

41   *The Times*, 24 February 1879.

42   *Ibid.*

43   *Ibid.*

44   Shore (ed.), *Trials of Charles Frederick Peace*, p.45 – Peace's written statement to the Home Office.

45   *The Times*, 26 February 1879.

46   *Ibid.*

47   *Ibid.* 3 March 1879.

48   *Ibid.*

49   *Ibid.*

50   Shore (ed.), *Trials of Charles Frederick Peace*, Peace's written confession, pp.44, 45.

51   *The Times*, 3 March 1879.

52   Hansard, HC Deb., 11 May 1886, Vol. 305, cc767-90.

53   *The Times*, 26 February 1879.

54   *The Times*, 28 February 1879; see also *The Times*, 20 March 1879.

55   *The Times*, 20 March 1879.

56   Shore (ed.), *Trials of Charles Frederick Peace*, pp.46, 47.

57   Adam, H. L., *The Police Encyclopaedia*, Vol.7, pp.35, 36; *The Times*, 6 March 1879; petition referred to in *The Times*, 5 March 1879.

58   Hansard, HC Deb., 27 February 1879, Vol. 243, c1840.

Chapter 31

59 Hansard, HC Deb., 17 March 1879, Vol. 244, cc1035-6; *The Times*, 18 March 1879.

60 Hansard, HC Deb., 17 March 1879, Vol. 244, cc1035-6; *The Times*, 18 March 1879.

61 *The Times*, 22 March 1879.

62 Borchard, E. M., *Convicting the Innocent*, p.93.

63 Bent, J., *Criminal Life: Reminiscences of Forty-Two Years as a Police Officer*, p.241.

64 *Ibid.* p.242.

65 *Ibid.* p.242.

66 *Ibid.* p.242.

67 *The Times*, 8 April 1879.

68 *The Times*, 20 March 1879.

69 *Ibid.*

70 *Ibid.*

71 Supplement to the *Evening Post*, Wellington, New Zealand, 17 May 1879.

72 *Ibid.*

73 *Ibid.*

74 *Ibid.*

75 *Ibid.*

76 *Ibid.*

77 *Ibid.*

78 *Ibid.*

79 *Sydney Morning Herald*, 16 May 1879.

80 *Ibid.*

81 *Ibid.*

82 *The Times*, 20 March 1879.

83 *Ibid.*

84 *Ibid.*

85 Supplement to the *Evening Post*, Wellington, New Zealand, 17 May 1879.

86 Hansard, HC Deb., 21 March 1879, Vol. 244, cc1430–2, Mr Richard Assheton Cross.

87 *The Times*, 20 February 1879.

88 Irving, H. B., *A Book of Remarkable Criminals*, 'The Life of Charles Peace', p.77.

Chapter 32

89 *The Times*, 27 February 1879.

90 *Ibid.*

91 *Ibid.*

92 *Ibid.*

93 *Ibid.*

94 *Ibid.*

95 Anon., *The Master Criminal. The Life Story of Charles Peace*, p.120.

96 *Ibid.* p.122.

97 *Ibid.* p.120.

98 Shore (ed.), *Trials of Charles Frederick Peace*, p.169.

99 Ward, D., *The King of the Lags*, pp.162, 172.

100 Original of document in Sheffield Archives. Anon., *The Master Criminal. The Life Story of Charles Peace*, p.122, states that he left it all divided between Hannah, his brother Daniel, his daughter and Willie, while Ward, D., *The King of the Lags*, p.172, says he left it all equally to Hannah and Willie.

101 *The Times*, 26 February 1879.

102 *Ibid*.

103 Shore (ed.), *Trials of Charles Frederick Peace*, p.169.

104 *The Times*, 26 February 1879.

105 Anon., *The Master Criminal. The Life Story of Charles Peace*, p.122.

106 *Ibid*. p.123.

107 Ward, D., *The King of the Lags*, p.114.

108 *Ibid*. p.174.

109 *The Times*, 26 February 1879.

110 *Ibid*.

111 *Ibid*.

112 *Ibid*.

113 This version is taken from *The Times*, 26 February 1879. Slightly varying versions of his last speech are given in Williams, M. S., *Leaves of a Life: Being the Reminiscences of Montagu Williams, Q.C.*, Vol. 2, p.130; Anon., *The Master Criminal. The Life Story of Charles Peace*, p.127; and Shore (ed.), *Trials of Charles Frederick Peace*, p.170.

114 This version is taken from *The Times*, 26 February 1879. Slightly varying versions of his last speech given in Williams, M. S., *Leaves of a Life: Being the Reminiscences of Montagu Williams, Q.C.*, Vol. 2, p.130; Anon., *The Master Criminal. The Life Story of Charles Peace*, p.127; Shore (ed.), *Trials of Charles Frederick Peace*, p.170.

115 *The Times*, 26 February 1879.

116 *Ibid*.

117 His certificate of death.

118 Griffiths, *Fifty Years of Public Service*, p.331.

119 Advertisement in *The Times*, 18 February 1879.

Select Bibliography

Adam, H. L., *The Police Encyclopaedia*, Vol. 7 (London: The Waverly Book Co., 1910).

Adam, H. L., *Police Work from Within: With some reflections upon women, the law and lawyers* (London: Holden and Hardingham, 1914).

Anon., *The Master Criminal. The Life Story of Charles Peace*, reprint of 1911 edition (Netherlands: Fredonia Books, 2004).

Bent, J., *Criminal Life: Reminiscences of Forty-Two Years as a Police Officer* (Manchester: J. Heywood, 1891).

Berrey, R. J. Power, *The Bye-ways of Crime with Some Stories from the Black Museum* (London: Greening and Co., 1899).

Birkenhead, F. E. Smith, Earl of, *Famous Trials of History* (London: Hutchinson, 1930).

Borchard, E. M., *Convicting the Innocent* (USA: Yale University Press, 1932).

Deans, R. S., *Notable Trials: Romances of the Law Courts* (London: Cassell, 1906).

Durston, G. J., *Burglars and Bobbies: Crime and Policing in Victorian London* (Newcastle upon Tyne: Cambridge Scholars Publishing, 2012).

Forster, J., *Studies in Black and Red* (London: Ward and Downey, 1896).

Gaskell, N. K., *The Romantic Career of a Great Criminal: A Memoir of Charles Peace* (London: N. K. Gaskell, 1906).

Griffiths, A., *Fifty Years of Public Service* (London: Cassell, 1904).

Griffiths, A., *Mysteries of Police and Crime*, 2 vols (London: Cassell, 1899).

Hale, L., *Hanged in Error* (London: Penguin, 1961).

Honeycombe, G., *Dark Secrets of the Black Museum, 1835–1985: more dark secrets from 150 years of the most notorious crimes in England* (London: John Blake, 2014).

Horsley, J. W., *How Criminals are Made and Prevented: A Retrospect of Forty years* (London: T. Fisher Unwin, 1912).

Irving, H. B., *A Book of Remarkable Criminals* (London: Cassell, 1918).

Lamb, F., *Forty Years in the Old Bailey* (London: Stevens and Sons, 1913).

Machan, P., 'The Fantastic Career of Charlie Peace 1831–1879', *Tales of Victorian Sheffield No. 1* (Sheffield: ALD Design & Print, 1999).

Morton, J., *Justice Denied, Extraordinary Miscarriages of Justice* (London: Robinson, 2015).

Parry, Sir E. A., *The Drama of the Law* (London: Unwin, 1924).

Postgate, R. W., *Murder, Piracy and Treason: a selection of notable English Trials* (London: Cape, 1925).

Shore, W. Teignmouth (ed.), *Trials of Charles Frederick Peace* (London: William Hodge, 1926).

Walbrook, H. M., *Murders and Murder Trials, 1812–1912* (London: Constable, 1932).

Ward, D., *The King of the Lags* (London: Elek Books, 1963).

Whibley, C., *A Book of Scoundrels* (London: Constable, 1911).

Williams, M. S., *Leaves of a Life: Being the Reminiscences of Montagu Williams QC*, Vol. 2 (London: Macmillan and Co., 1890).

Index

If you enjoyed this book, you may also be interested in…

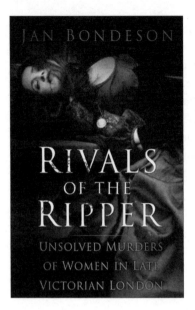

Rivals of the Ripper: Unsolved Murders of Women in Late Victorian London

JAN BONDESON

978 0 7509 6425 8

When discussing unsolved murders of women in late Victorian London, most people think of the depredations of Jack the Ripper. But he was just one of a string of phantom murderers whose unsolved slayings outraged late Victorian Britain. The mysterious Great Coram Street, Burton Crescent and Euston Square murders were talked about with bated breath, and the northern part of Bloomsbury got the unflattering nickname of the 'murder neighbourhood' for its profusion of unsolved mysteries. Marvel at the convoluted Kingswood Mystery, littered with fake names and mistaken identities; be puzzled by the blackmail and secret marriage in the Cannon Street Murder; and shudder at the vicious yet silent killing in St Giles that took place in a crowded house in the dead of night. This book is the first to resurrect these unsolved Victorian murder mysteries, and to highlight the ghoulish handiwork of the Rivals of the Ripper: the spectral killers of gas-lit London.

'Sparkles with new research and exciting discoveries. A tour de force.'

Richard Whittington-Egan, author of *Jack the Ripper: The Definitive Casebook*

'A must-have volume for all aficionados of the true crime genre and an entertaining book for the general reader. Set to become a touchstone work.'

Stewart P. Evans

The
History
Press

The destination for history
www.thehistorypress.co.uk